Praise for
Bring the WORLD to Your Classroom

"I've always had a fondness for maps and traveling—and through this book by Kelly and Kim we can bring both into our classrooms in powerful new ways. Leveraging the opportunities provided by Google Geo tools, students can explore and interact with the world with little more than a screen and an internet connection. Packed with tips, tricks, and ideas, this is a practical guide for any teacher hoping to set her students free on a global adventure!"

—**Jennie Magiera**, author of Corwin bestseller *Courageous Edventures*

"I believe *Bring the World to Your Classroom* is an incredible, streamlined guide for anyone interested in applying Google Geo tools in their educational practice. In our dynamic world, we need to empower students to conduct research towards solving problems in their local communities, collaborate beyond the walls of the classroom, and learn how to make informed decisions that have powerful ripple effects around the world. On a daily basis, educators play such a profound role on positive global impact, but it can be difficult to navigate all the resources available. *Bring the World to Your Classroom* helps solve that challenge by bridging technology, pedagogy, amazing tips, and the realities of the classroom to help create immersive learning experiences for all."

—**Emily Henderson**, program manager, Google Earth Education

"Kelly and Kim have created the go-to guide connecting Google Geo Tools to the classroom for engaging, impactful lessons. One chapter in and I'm already inspired to create new lessons that transform learning past the walls of my classroom. *Bring the World to Your Classroom* not only explains how to design these lessons, it illustrates the ease with which educators can integrate authentic global learning into their curriculum. This is a book that you will be referring back to many times as you begin creating!"

—**Lisa Highfill**, teacher and coauthor of *The HyperDoc Handbook*

"*Bring the World to Your Classroom* has left me excited and curious about using the many Google Geo tools. This isn't just another how-to book. With this book, it's obvious Kelly and Kim have poured their hearts into helping educators have access to practical and proven work. I love how they've crafted step-by-step tools to recreate classroom magic with Google Geo tools."

—**Chris Scott**, learning guru and author of *Minecraft Lab for Kids*

"Kim and Kelly have put together the ultimate resource for meaningful, effective use of Google's Geo tools in your classroom. It's the perfect balance of the 'how-to,' pedagogy, and practical application that shows teachers how to design lessons to 'take' their class anywhere in the world. All teachers should read this book to understand all of the possibilities!"

—**Kyle Pace**, director of technology, Grain Valley
School District (Grain Valley, MO)

"A must-have book for any K–12 educator looking to incorporate Google Geo Tools such as My Maps, Google Maps, Tour Builder, or virtual reality for impactful learning. The step-by-step instructions make it easy for the first-time users, while the pro tips are especially useful for the experienced users."

—**Kavita Gupta**, teacher, AP Chemistry, Fremont Union
High School District (Cupertino, CA)

"Kelly and Kim give so many authentic and practical ideas for using Google tools in classrooms. These descriptive and real-life learning experiences can only help students retain and recall the information they need and apply technology to solve problems."

—**Corin Wyatt**, director of technology and
innovation, Forest Grove School District (Forest Grove, OR)

"As a former history teacher, I love that Kelly and Kim have made geography accessible for teachers everywhere. From step-by-step tutorials to the all-important 'What You Can Do Tomorrow' sections, so many tools and tricks are made easy by this book. Plus, they highlighted my favorite under-utilized student creation tool in Google Drive: My Maps!"

—**Karl Lindgren-Streicher**, vice principal at Westview
Secondary School (British Columbia, Canada)

"Kelly and Kim created an EduAwesome resource for global-minded educators. They found the perfect balance between sharing and explaining tools, sharing the sound pedagogy behind those tools, and giving concrete examples to implement the next day. Educators new to tech as well as experts will find tools, tricks, and lessons that will change their classrooms and their schools."

—**Bill Selak**, billselak.com

"Educators have the unique opportunity to provide students with experiences that develop their local and global lenses. Kelly and Kim have brought their passion for doing so to their book, *Bring the World to Your Classroom*. They have taken their classroom experience and coupled it with their tool know-how to provide a simple, easy-to-follow book on creating these important experiences."

—**Kristina Ishmael-Peters**, public interest technology and education policy fellow, New America

"I was the child who flipped through each new *National Geographic* to find the map. I could pore over the map for hours: new places, new ideas, exploring the world in my living room. With that said, 'The Why' of Kim and Kelly's book was an immediate hook for me. Our world is changing rapidly. It feels both very, very large and very small at the same time. For our students, developing a meaningful understanding of geography will build informed, involved, and compassionate citizens. This book will help educators not only see geography's role in all aspects of teaching and learning, but also support their use of Geo Tools to put the world in student's hands. When we connect our learning to the actual places and people on the globe, we help children see our interconnectedness, our similarities, and our differences. The directions for teachers are clear, the classroom examples are pertinent, and the inclusion of multiple platforms will make this useful for many learning environments. *Bring the World to Your Classroom* will be in my teachers' hands right away!"

—**Catina Haugen**, principal, Petaluma City Schools (Petaluma, CA)

"When educators are introduced to the host of Geo Tools offered by Google, they quickly realize how many ways these tools can be used to enhance the curriculum. In this book, Kelly and Kim provide a comprehensive overview and 'how-to' for each of the tools, from Google Street View to Google Story Spheres. In addition, they include practical and easy-to-implement ideas for use of these powerful tools in the classroom. This book would be perfect as the basis for an educator study group or PLC!"

—**Kathy Schrock** (@kathyschrock), educational technologist

Kelly Kermode   Kim Randall

Bring the WORLD to Your Classroom

Using Google Geo Tools

Bring the World to Your Classroom
© 2018 by Kelly Kermode and Kim Randall

This book is available at special discounts when purchased in quantity for use as premiums, promotions, fundraising, and educational use. For inquiries and details, contact the publisher at press@edtechteam.com.

Google and the Google logo are registered trademarks of Google Inc.

Published by EdTechTeam Press
Cover Design by Genesis Kohler
Interior Design by My Writers' Connection

TPB ISBN: 978-1-945167-41-6
Ebook ISBN: 978-1-945167-42-3
Library of Congress Control Number: 2017961256
First Printing: February 2018

Irvine, California

Contents

FOREWORD by Rushton Hurley

There's something about a map. A map can reveal somewhere you've never visited, hint of exciting possibilities, and give us momentary or lifelong purpose.

The two women who crafted this book—this map to all sorts of educational treasures—are talented, thoughtful, and accomplished educators I have known for many years. Follow this map to possibilities that will be both practical and inspiring!

Maps have always inspired me. They did so when I was a child, and they do so for me in my ever-changing role as an educator.

One might argue that a teacher's primary job is inspiring students to see something new within themselves. Many of our students, though, may step into our classrooms having never traveled beyond their hometowns and neighborhoods. They see videos and programs about other places, but the passive experience of simply being a viewer lacks much of the perspective-changing excitement that comes from choosing one's own path and discovering new territories for oneself.

I recall my first views of the trees around Cape Town, of the wild parrots along the coast west of Melbourne, of the Roman and Byzantine ruins of Istanbul, and of the vibrant communities within the slums built on top of each other in Mumbai.

For many years, I took groups of students to Japan to try out the language skills they were learning in my class, and vividly recall their reactions to the palpable history of Kyoto and the chants of the monks in a temple on Mt. Koya. These trips were opportunities to take students to places that inspired me, and then to watch as the magic of these places inspired my students.

For teachers without ready opportunities to take students to new places, however, the last decade has seen all sorts of geography-related tools appear that can allow any educator to excite a child's imagination.

This brings us to now—the moment in which you hold a book designed to help you inspire.

Kermode and Randall have gathered for you some of the most promising and powerful of these tools, adding plenty of information on how to use them, suggesting activities for their use in your homes and classrooms, and linking to resources to expand learning yet further.

The focus is on the many active possibilities of these tools for exploring the world. Gone, thankfully, is the time when the best we could do was start a video to learn of another place. Now students can choose which streets to explore, see changes over time, pull together information in maps they create, share ideas with their peers on the other side of the world, and much more.

You will find this compact introduction one that creates many possibilities for you and your students. May you also find yourself inspired by all the magical potential of these incredible tools.

DEDICATIONS

From Kelly

To my children, Tynan and Madeleine: You show me how to see the world differently every day.

To my parents, Ken and Shyle Kermode: Thank you for your support throughout the years. I realize it may not be easy to have your daughter gallivanting all over the earth, but you've always encouraged me to follow the adventures that speak to me ... Thank you.

From Kim

To my parents, Gale and Howard Randall: Thank you for the opportunities and experiences to explore the globe starting at a very young age. My love for traveling the earth, geography, cultures, teaching, and photography stem from our travels as a family. Without your love, support, understanding, and encouragement, none of this would have been possible.

To JTG: So happy you're on this journey with me. Just show up.

PREFACE

Taking a small cue from the d.school at Stanford, we are bringing you the preface in the Why, How, and What format. Although this book has a focus on the tools (the what), and how you can use them in your classroom, our main why for this book is to share our passion for global education and bringing people together in immersive learning experiences. We hope that when you understand the why, this book becomes a conduit for you to take your great teaching practices and marry them with geo-based activities to create strong global citizens.

Enjoy.

THE WHY

The landscape of our communities has changed. We no longer simply live in the small towns or big cities of our childhoods, because no matter where our homes are, we are all part of a global community. Within this expansive community, our actions, direct and indirect, affect the lives of others around the world. As educators, it is our responsibility to make sure our students understand the impact and interaction they have and can have on communities near and far.

As teachers, we know we must cover certain content standards and intentionally build specific skills. But for our students to contribute back to our global community and have strong employability skills, educational practices must also evolve. We must provide students with opportunities to experience the kind of process-driven, constantly improving workflow offered by the modern technology tools. Which is why the days of having students color paper maps to demonstrate global knowledge are over. It's also why map printing companies are suffering and folding (pun intended). In their stead, geo tools such as Google Maps, Waze, Google Earth, Google Street View, Companion, and other dynamic mapping apps claim an increasingly larger user base. These constantly updating tools can meet learners' needs by staying current with their content and delivery in a way that the maps we used as children never could.

Our students are accustomed to working with dynamic informational sources. These ephemeral informational highways are part of the landscape in which the younger generations are growing up. There is no stagnation when it comes to geography and anthropology. In the past decade alone, there have been more than thirty changes to countries and capitals around the world. Today's students have the opportunity to work with content using tools that allow for a global lens that expands and adapts to mirror the world's current state. Additionally, these tools encourage students to tap into higher levels of learning, including creating and evaluating. With these types of dynamic tools at the forefront of learning for students, classroom learning is shifting from silos of recall and remembering to fluid learning environments wherein students create, examine different points of view, and justify their thinking through modeling and data sourcing.

The idea of the global community and an interwoven economy is not new. Thomas Friedman first published *The World Is Flat* in 2005—yes, more than ten years ago. The message his book conveys is one of a growing global market and leveled playing field for economic gain. He drives home the point that several shifts, including political, economic, and technological, have "flattened" the global markets, creating new opportunities for many people around the globe. He advocated for education to make the changes necessary to get ahead of the shift and prepare children for the world they are facing. Now, years later, we are still working towards that shift. We are still trying to create learning environments that are student centered and focused on developing the whole child.

Children are growing up in a world of exponential change and technological advancement. With that reality comes another: Some experts predict that our global population will reach around ten billion by 2050. With an exploding population comes an increase in pollution, unsustainable resource demands, disease management, water conservation, and natural resource allocations. Our students will need to be able to communicate and collaborate beyond borders to solve some of these tough challenges facing our global community.

We, as educators and parents, must help guide the next generation to become aware of their personal role in our global environment. Likewise, we must prepare them with the skills that employers and community leaders demand, such as the ability to aggregate data, see trends, understand global context, and apply solutions. Through experience and research, we (the authors) have learned that using dynamic geo tools and offering students greater opportunities for collaboration, communication, critical thinking, and creativity fosters the development of strong global citizens. No matter what content area or grade level you teach, we urge you to share in the responsibility of developing resourceful, empathetic citizens. Together, we can equip the next generation to help make our world a better place for everyone.

THE HOW

In this book you will find tools, tricks, and tips that you can implement to shift your own classroom pedagogy towards a more global-community-minded approach. We have chosen to take a deep-dive approach by focusing on a few tools and offering a selection of alternatives for further learning and exploring.

Here is a brief list of some of the activities we'll be covering in this book:

» Explore mapping in new ways with Google Maps and My Maps

» Combine storytelling with maps using Tour Builder

» Build immersive learning experiences with Street View, Google Earth, and Google Cardboard

» Create interactive tours using Google Earth

» Curate information using open data sources and visualize it using Google Maps

» Collaborate with other classrooms and experts using Google Hangouts and YouTube

» Provide a wealth of extra resources you can take to your students to foster their creativity and critical thinking

THE WHAT

If our students are going to thrive in the global community, they must develop specific competencies. By using Google's geo tools and open data sources in your classroom, you are choosing to give your students the necessary global context that will shape the rest of their learning.

» Students will grow their awareness of geography and geospatial reasoning. By using mapping tools and open data, students can find connections between themselves and the rest of world as well as see commonalities and differences from continent to continent.

» Through creating maps and viewing immersive imagery and video, students will own their learning about landforms and the environment through inquiry and creation.

» Students will also develop an empathy for other cultures. By offering the opportunity to interact with other classrooms around the world, students can practice dialoguing with others while learning about their cultures, traditions, and surroundings.

In short, your students will learn to thrive as community members on a local as well as an international scale. They will know how to navigate the global land-scape. Students will become global citizens who are able to find their own place in our world and discover how they can bring good to the greater whole.

 For more information on standards and global competencies, please visit:

» geotools.co/standards

CHAPTER 1:
Build Geographical Awareness using My Maps

Ms. Mauro, a grade-one teacher in Canada, wanted a more interesting way to teach her young students about the change of seasons. She also wanted to use tools that would allow her students to collaborate, communicate, and share their learning, both with other students and with a global audience. So, using Google My Maps, she had her students observe and capture the changes of their environment throughout the year.

Each of Ms. Mauro's students picked out a tree in their community to watch how it changed throughout the year. With My Maps and Google Drive, she created and shared a class My Map that her students could edit. She placed a marker on the map where each student's tree was located. Then, throughout the year, her students made observations, took pictures or drew their trees, and added their collected data and images to their marker on the class My Map.

Ms. Mauro embedded the My Maps on a Google Site to allow other classes, parents, family members, and friends to see the progress of seasonal changes (of the trees) throughout the year. Ms. Mauro took the project a step further by inviting a class in another region of the country to participate and collaborate with her class by using the sharing and editing features of My Maps and Google Apps.

The year-long project allowed students to discuss weather conditions with a class from a different location and compare and contrast changes in the environment. By using My Maps, Ms. Mauro's students became creators of content, not just consumers.

MY MAPS: An Overview

One of the ways students can begin to develop connections between the community they live in and the rest of the world is by exploring and developing an understanding of the relationship of self to community on a global scale. Creating their own maps is a step toward this understanding.

My Maps is a Google app that was added into Google Drive in the summer of 2015. This addition allows My Maps to be saved in Google Drive along with other student documents and work, which makes them easy to find.

My Maps allows a user to customize maps by choosing a variety of options to display information, including markers, adding images and video, drawing shapes, measuring distances, and finding directions. Additionally, users can import data (places) into the map from a spreadsheet. Multiple layers of locations and information can be a part of the map. Once created, My Maps saves into Google Drive and can be opened in Google Maps, embedded into a webpage, shared as a collaborative map, or exported as KML files for use in Google Earth. The opportunities for using My Maps in the classroom are endless. Let's take a look:

Explore the World

At its simplest level, My Maps can be used to show students the map of the world. My Maps opens in "Map" view as a standard map background. There are nine Base Map views from which to choose. These can be changed at any time by clicking "Base Map" at the bottom of the layer list. The current base map options are Map, Satellite, Terrain, Light Political, Mono City, Simple Atlas, Light Landmass, Dark Landmass, and Whitewater. Some ways to use the different base maps views include the following:

» Use the Map view for details of street and location names

» Use the Terrain map to study topography

» Use the Atlas map to study countries and geography

» Use the Satellite map for a world imagery view

» Use the Mono City map to study travel from place to place and distance measuring

» Use alternative views for stylized effects (Light/Dark Landmass maps and the Whitewater map)

My Maps Quick Tutorial

Getting started with My Maps begins with logging into your Google account. (My Maps will work with both a G Suite account and a personal Google account.) There are three ways to get to My Maps:

FIGURE 1.1

1. Open Google Drive (FIGURE 1.1), Click on New, scroll down to More, select Google My Maps (FIGURE 1.2).

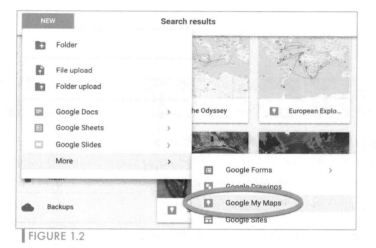

FIGURE 1.2

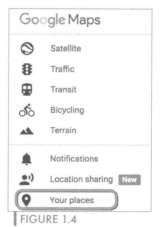

FIGURE 1.4

2. Go to the address mymaps.google.com and click on Create a New Map in the upper left side of the page (FIGURE 1.3). On this page you will also see all maps owned by the user, not owned by the user, shared by and to the user, and recent maps with which the user has worked.

FIGURE 1.3

3. Go to maps.google.com (Google Maps website) and in the upper left corner click on the menu icon. Scroll down and click on Your Places in the window that appears (FIGURE 1.4). Navigate all the way to the right and click on Maps. At the bottom, click on Create.

PRO TIP: Options one and two are easiest for students to find and use. Adding the My Maps link to student bookmarks is another way to make it easy for them to find.

Once opened, a new My Maps will be named an Untitled Map. It is a good idea to rename the map right away to make it easier to find in Google Drive later. To rename the map, click in the words Untitled Map and type the new name.

By default, My Maps opens with one layer. This layer is also an Untitled Layer. Think of layers as categories of information that will be displayed on the map. A layer title can be added when you create the map, or it can be added later; however, if you or your students plan to have more than one layer on a map, it is a good idea to title each layer. To title the layer, click in the box that says Untitled Layer and type the new name of the layer into the box.

Using Layers to Display Information

By using layers in My Maps, your students can build projects with multiple data sets. For reference, explore the examples below.

Students studying Westward Expansion can create a My Map with a layer for various topics that had an impact on the movement west. There may be layers dealing with environmental concerns, food shortages, human interactions/events/meetings, fights/battles, as well as places of settlement.

If your students are studying natural disasters, they may wish to create respective layers for tornadoes, earthquakes, and hurricanes. Once the data has been plotted, students may find it interesting to toggle each layer's checkbox to turn them off from view. They then can import or map a fourth layer with plate tectonics and locations of all the fault lines in the world. After this, they turn back on the natural disaster layers and can draw inferences about the correlations between the different map layers.

Working with Markers

My Maps has a lot of creation features for building a map. The first feature to explore is markers. These markers can be added in a couple of ways:

1. Starting with the search bar at the top of the map, (FIGURE 1.5) type the name of a place or an address you would like to add to your map. Your search results will appear on the map and to the left as a list of green

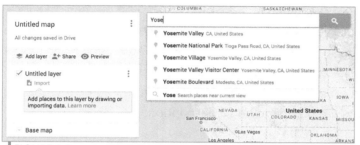

FIGURE 1.5

place markers (FIGURE 1.6). There are two ways to add that location to become part of your My Map: If you hover over the listing on the left, you'll see a [+] symbol. Also, if you click on the desired location, an info card will pop up. On the bottom left corner of the info card, you will see another [+] symbol next to Add to Map. Either of these options work, and once you click on one to add the place to your map, the marker will change from green to blue and will be added to your layer on the left (FIGURE 1.7).

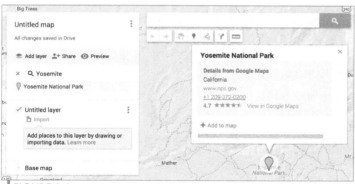

FIGURE 1.6

FIGURE 1.7

PRO TIP: Using longitude/latitude coordinates in the white search bar will also find a location, and it can then be added to a layer. Having trouble finding coordinates? Try searching for the location in Google Maps (maps.google.com). Once found, look in the address bar, scroll to the right, and the coordinates should be there. Or right click on a placemark in Google Maps and click "What's here?" This will show the longitude/latitude.

2. Another way to add markers to the map is to *drop* them on the map. Use the +/- tools to zoom in and out on the map and navigate to a location where you would like to drop a marker. In the toolbar found below the search bar, find and click on the Add Marker icon (FIGURE 1.8). Your cursor will change to a + symbol. Click on the desired location on the map to drop a marker. In the info card that pops up, name the place and add a description.

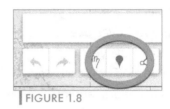

FIGURE 1.8

Marker Customization

When you have a list of locations in a layer, you can customize the markers in a number of ways:

» Change the marker icon/color

» Add a custom icon

» Edit marker data

» Add photos and videos to a marker

» Stylize markers

Change a Marker Icon or Color

Changing a marker icon or color can be done in two ways:

1. In the layer list, hover over the location with your mouse until a paint bucket appears (FIGURE 1.9). Click the paint bucket to see the icon

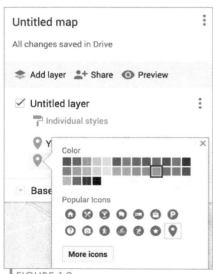

FIGURE 1.9

and color options. Click on the More icons button for additional shapes, symbols, and icons.

2. You can click on the marker on the map which opens the info card. Click on the paint bucket icon and follow the same steps above.

Add a Custom Icon

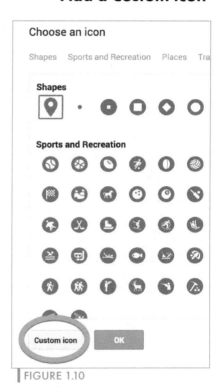

FIGURE 1.10

Adding a custom icon can also be done by selecting the paint bucket icon and clicking on the More icons button. Click on the Custom icon button to import an image of your choice. You will see the following options (FIGURE 1.10):

» **Upload**—Upload an image from a computer.

» **WebCam**—Use the webcam on the computer to take an image picture.

» **Image URL**—Use an image from the web. (Find the URL and copy/paste it in the space provided.)

» **Your Photos**—Use images uploaded to Google Photos.

» **Google Drive**—Use images from your Google Drive.

» **Google Image Search**—Search the Web for an image to use.

 PRO TIP: When searching for a custom icon, add the word icon to your search and your search results will yield a whole new array of options; for example, instead of just searching "beach," try searching "beach icon." The results improve significantly when you specify what you are searching for.

Edit Marker Data

A marker label or description can be edited at any time. To do so, click on the marker to make the info card appear. Select the pencil (edit) icon to edit or update the marker label and description (FIGURE 1.11).

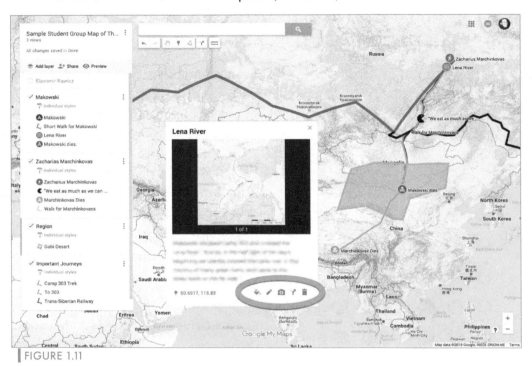

FIGURE 1.11

Add Photos and Videos to a Marker

Adding images and videos to a marker is a great way for students to elaborate or visually display a location. By clicking on the marker on the map, the info card appears. This time click on the camera icon at the bottom of the card. The current options to add an image/video include the following:

» **Upload**—Upload an image from a computer.

» **WebCam**—Use the webcam on the computer to take an image picture.

» **Image URL**—Use an image from the web. (Find the URL and copy/paste it in the space provided.)

» **Your Photos**—Use images uploaded to Google Photos.

» **Google Drive**—Use images from your Google Drive.

» **Google Image Search**—Search the Web for an image to use by typing in the topic for which you are looking. When an option you like appears, click on the image to insert it.

PRO TIP: Adding an animated gif also works.

» **YouTube Search**—Type in a topic and look for a video.

» **YouTube URL**—Search for a video at youtube.com, upload/edit/create your own video, or use a video already in your favorites/playlist. Simply copy and paste the YouTube link into the bar.

Stylizing Markers

In addition to customizing markers, another marker customization option is to stylize how the markers appear on the map as well as in the layer. By default, a layer starts out with Individual Styles. Clicking on the word's Individual Styles will open a window with the following options:

Changing how places are grouped

» Uniform Style (all the same maker)

» Sequence of colors and letters

» Individual Styles

» Style by data column title (FIGURE 1.12)

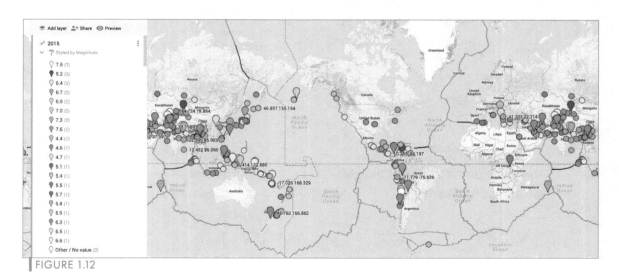

FIGURE 1.12

Using marker styles to visualize data on the map

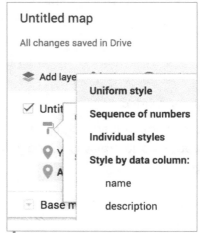

FIGURE 1.13

Stylizing markers can be useful depending on the type of data displayed on the map; for example, if students plot recent volcanoes and earthquakes on the same layer, stylizing will let them show both, but as separate colored markers. Or if students are mapping animal migration, they may choose to assign marker styles based on the type of animal so that all the birds have the same marker icon, and other animal groups get assigned their own marker style as well (FIGURE 1.13).

The Data behind the Scenes

While you are building a map layer with markers, My Maps works behind the scenes to create a data table by collecting the information in the markers. To display the data table for a layer, click on the menu icon (three dots) beside the title of the layer. From the options presented, click on Open data table (FIGURE 1.14).

The data table displays the information in the markers and allows you to make the following updates or changes:

» Editing or updating typos

» Sorting data in the columns

» Adding or deleting columns (which display in the info cards)

» Duplicating a column

» Using a column to set as a title (the title on the info cards)

FIGURE 1.14

Working with Line/Shape Tool

Another feature of My Maps is the ability to draw lines and polygons (shapes) on the map. Students can use this tool to outline an area on the map, measure the area and perimeter of a location, and even compare sizes of continents, countries, states, and cities.

To explore this feature, we recommend adding a new layer specifically for lines and shapes. Click on Add layer and name the new layer.

NOTE: Before you begin working on your map, check to be sure you are working on the right layer. To determine which layer is currently selected, look on the left edge of the layer menu. The active layer will be indicated by a blue line along the left edge of its box. To choose a different layer on which to work, simply click anywhere in the desired layer's box (FIGURE 1.15).

FIGURE 1.15

PRO TIP: If a student accidentally adds a marker to a layer but it belongs in another layer, the markers can be dragged and dropped in between layers. To do this, click on the item to be moved in the layer list and drag it to the desired layer.

FIGURE 1.16

To use the *Draw a line* tool, click on the icon found in the toolbar below the search box and select *Add a line or shape* from the menu that appears (FIGURE 1.16). Once selected, the cursor will change to a plus symbol (+). Click anywhere on the map, then move the cursor to begin a line. Click again to add a new section of line or to change directions. Continue moving the cursor and clicking to extend the line. To end the line, double click on the endpoint. An info card will pop up with a line number (e.g., Line 1). Click in the title bar to rename the line and then click Save. Once the info card is saved, the distance of the line will be selected. This tool allows students to easily find measurements on the map.

Using the same drawing tool, students can also create shapes called polygons in My Maps. As they use the line tool and click on the map to draw the line, each point will be connected. To complete the shape, click on the starting point of the line. Once again, an info card pops up with a generic title provided for the new shape (e.g., Polygon 1). Click in the title bar of the info card to rename the shape and then click Save. Once saved, the shape's area and perimeter appear at the bottom of the info card, bringing math into maps with geometry and real-world situations (FIGURE 1.17).

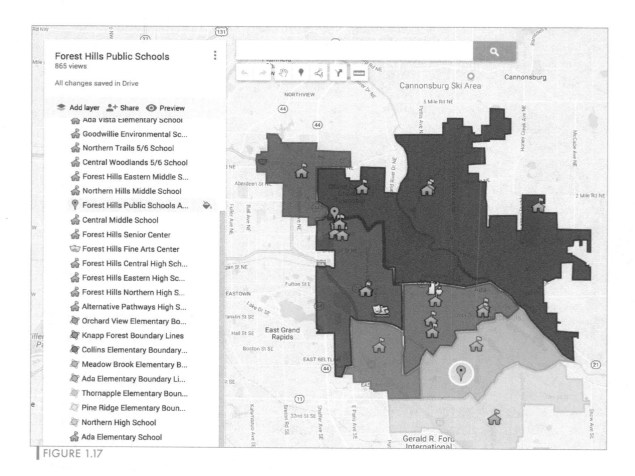

FIGURE 1.17

The colors of the lines and shapes can be changed and customized the same way markers are changed, with the paint bucket icon. Either hover your cursor over the line or shape in the layer or click on the line or shape to bring up the info card. Click on the paint bucket icon to open the menu of color choices as well as slider bars for changing the line thickness and transparency of shapes.

No free-form drawing tool is currently available in My Maps. Nor is it possible to lock shapes in place on the map. However, once a shape is drawn, it is possible to click the corner points and drag to adjust the shape and size.

Using Visualization to Help Students Grasp Mapping Distortions

Because our world is spherical and maps are flat, a distortion occurs. This distortion is the most prominent near the north and south poles. To help students grasp the true size of land masses, country sizes, and other geographical landmarks, we can use the polygon tool for an interactive experience.

Shapes and lines can be moved (dragged) anywhere on the map. To move a shape, click once on the shape to select it and then click and drag the shape to a new location. This feature allows students to visually compare the size of different geographical locations. Comparison exercises are especially impactful when students are looking at the upper part of the northern hemisphere and lower part of the southern hemisphere where the shapes change size in correlation to the projection (curvature) of the earth. This visual activity fosters inquiry and leads to conversations about this phenomenon (FIGURE 1.18).

For details and sample maps for this, please visit geotools.co/poly.

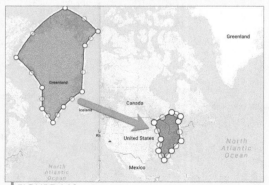

FIGURE 1.18

Measuring Features

FIGURE 1.19

My Maps provides a ruler tool (FIGURE 1.19) (located in the toolbar below the search bar). This ruler can be used to measure any distances or areas on the map. Click on the ruler and then hover your cursor over the map. The cursor will change to a plus symbol (+). When you click on the map and move your mouse, you'll notice that distance measurements will appear. (Fun fact: Measurements will automatically change on the map depending on the country in which you are located, e.g., US = miles, Canada = kilometers). The ruler can also be used to measure areas by connecting the lines back to the starting point. This measurement will only stay on the map until you click elsewhere, as it is not a permanent drawing.

PRO TIP: If at any time you are stuck on the map, click the hand icon to get your cursor back. There are also undo and redo arrows (FIGURE 1.20) in case you delete something accidentally. Currently, there is no revision history like what you can find with other G Suite Tools.

FIGURE 1.20

Creating Directions and Routes

Never has it been to so easy to plot directions or routes as it is with modern mapping tools. In My Maps, for example, you can create directions/routes in a variety of ways, including driving, bicycling, and walking. Any time a new set of directions or routes is created, it is automatically started in a new layer on My Map.

FIGURE 1.21

To create directions with existing markers on the map, click on a marker on the map. When the info card pops up, click on the Directions icon (FIGURE 1.21). This will create a new Directions layer and will list the location you've selected as A. Click on another marker on the map to add it to the Directions layer as location B. If these are out of order for your desired starting and ending points, simply click on the location in the Directions layer and drag it up or down to change the directions/route order.

To add locations to the directions layer, click on Add Destination in the Directions layer to add the next location. The route (indicated by a blue line) will update on the map. My Maps allows ten destinations in one direction/route layer.

To change or customize a route on My Map, click on the blue route line. A circle will appear on the line. Drag this circle to change the route.

It is also possible to change the type of directions in the layer from driving to bicycling or walking. Students can compare how long it takes to travel using these various modes of transportation. This tool can be used to plot routes of book characters or historical figures. It can even be used to track animal routes or migration patterns.

Directions/routes can also be created using the Draw a line tool. Click on this icon and select Add a driving route (or biking or walking route). This will open a new layer with blank spaces for A to B. Click in A and type in a location. Click in B and type in another location. The directions will populate on the map. Using this method, directions and routes can be to anywhere on the map and are not limited to markers already in a layer.

In addition to creating the route on the map, the Directions layer allows users to see step-by-step directions and estimated travel time. To access these instructions, click on the three-dot menu in the upper right corner of the Directions layer. From the options that appear, select Step-by-step directions to open a window that shows the total distance, estimate time, and turn-by-turn directions.

PRO TIP: The three-dot menu appears throughout G Suite for Education. When you see it, click on the menu to see what features are available.

Importing Data

We have looked at ways to place items (markers, images/videos, lines/shapes, directions) in My Maps with the tools in the toolbar.

Another unique and extremely useful feature of My Maps is the ability to import data into a layer and have My Maps plot or "drop" the markers on the map. This means our students can collect their own data.

PRO TIP: Importing data is easy to do using Google Forms and Google Sheets, or find sets of data to import to see visually on a map. For a tutorial on how to use Google Forms with Google My Maps, please visit **geotools.co/formtomap**.

The first step to importing data is to collect, find, or create some data. Data can be imported in the following file formats: CSV, TSV, KML, KMZ, GPX, or XLSX file, or a Google Sheet. The most commonly used data sources for students and teachers are likely to be a sheet from Google Sheets, CSV, or XLSX.

When preparing to import data, it is important to remember these require-ments:

> » At least one column in the sheet must contain one of these types of geographic information:
>> » Address
>> » Place name
>> » Latitude and Longitude
>> This is important because it allows My Maps to know where to drop the marker on the map when the information is imported.

> » No more than 2,000 rows of data per layer. If you have more than 2,000 rows of data, split them into two (or more) spreadsheets and import each sheet as a different layer.

> » The first row must contain the column titles (FIGURE 1.22).

When the data is ready for importing, head back to the My Maps map, add another layer, and rename it. When the new layer is added, a yellow box will

	Timestamp	Gender Idenification	What is your favorite city in the world?	Why is it your favorite place?	What is your last name?
2	8/30/2017 13:13:55	Female	Mabou, Cape Breton	It's tiny, but full of culture.	Kimove
3	8/30/2017 13:13:57	Male	Seoul	the food is awesome	McLean
4	8/30/2017 13:14:35	Female	Prague	The architecture, people and food!	Pretty
5	8/30/2017 13:14:51	Male	Melbourne	Amazing culture and climate	Rolfe

FIGURE 1.22

appear with the word *Import* above it. When you click on Import, a window will appear prompting you to choose a file to import. Navigate to find and select the file on your computer or in your Google Drive.

The rest of the importing process consists of selecting which column(s) in the sheet to use as the location to place the markers on the map. Check the box for which information My Maps should use. The final step is to select which column is used to title the markers (this can be changed once imported). Click Finish, and My Maps will use the spreadsheet to import the data and place the markers on the map. Here are a few things to remember:

» The layer created by the import in My Maps will be titled the name of the spreadsheet. Click in the layer title to change it.

» The markers will import as Uniform Style. Click the small arrow next to the words Uniform Style to see all locations.

» Click on Uniform Style to restyle the placemarks as described on page 10.

"We live in a wonderful world that is full of beauty, charm, and adventure. There is no end to the adventures we can have if only we seek them with our eyes open."

—Jawaharlal Nehru

NOTE: The first time you import a file, the browser (Chrome, in this example) will need permission to access files from Google Drive. There are a couple of ways to do this:

1. As importing starts, an Allow pop-up prompt will appear in the Chrome browser's omnibox (white search box). Click Allow.

2. Alternatively, this can be done in the Chrome browser settings.

   a. Make sure you are signed into Chrome.

   b. Navigate to the three-dot menu in the upper right corner of your Chrome browser.

   c. Click on Settings and scroll to the bottom of the menu.

   d. Click on Advanced.

   e. Under the Privacy and security menu click on Content settings.

   f. Scroll to Popups and click to open the menu.

   g. To allow My Maps to access Google Drive, click on Add beside the section titled Allow, then type "google.com/maps/d" into the Add a site box.

Sharing and Publishing a My Map

Collaborative maps are great for group work and class projects. My Maps has sharing and collaborating features similar to the other apps in G Suite for Education.

FIGURE 1.23

To share your map, click on the Share icon (FIGURE 1.23) to view the available sharing options, which include email, social media, and sharing a link where your map can be viewed or edited. If you choose to use the link option and would like collaborators to have the power to make additions or changes, remember to change the setting to Anyone with the link so others can edit the map.

Preview Your Map

The eye icon (FIGURE 1.24) allows you to see how the map will open in Google Maps.

Across from the title of the My Maps is another set of three dots. Clicking here brings up a number of other options, which include the following (FIGURE 1.25):

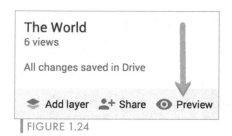

FIGURE 1.24

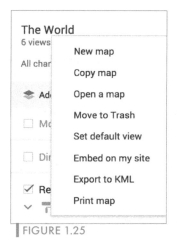

FIGURE 1.25

» **New map**—Start a new map.

» **Copy map**—Copy the current map.

» **Open a map**—Open an existing map.

» **Move to Trash**—Delete the map.

» **Set default view**—Determine how the map will open for viewers.

» **Embed on my site**—Publish your map on a website or blog by copying the embed code and pasting it on your site. To use this feature, your map's sharing settings must be set to Public on the web.

» **Export to KML**—A KML file is one that Google Earth uses. This can be used to open the map in Google Earth.

» **Print map**

PRO TIP: My Maps doesn't currently have a revision history feature, so be cautious about whom you invite to edit. If you want to keep an "original" copy of a My Map, use the Copy map feature to make a copy, and it will save in Drive before allowing others to edit. To Copy a My Map, click the three-dot menu next to the title of the map and select Copy map, and name the copy (FIGURE 1.25).

Finding My Maps Projects

Once you and your students have started to create content, finding My Maps projects is much like finding other Google Drive content. At times, you and your students will need to know how to navigate Drive and use search skills. My Maps projects can be found in several ways.

My Maps automatically saves as you work in Google Drive. You can find your map in Drive using the following methods:

Search for the title of the map in your Google Drive.

Click on Recent if it is a map that has been recently created/worked on or updated.

FIGURE 1.26

In the search bar, search by file type. Type "type:map," and your map files will show (FIGURE 1.26).

Open mymaps.google.com and find the map from the grid view or list view.

Search Google Maps (please see page 34 in the Google Maps section).

Search for others' created content on the web. (Please see geotools.co/kmzsearch for details.)

My Maps Apps

My Maps is available as a mobile app on Android devices from the Google Play store. On iOS devices, My Maps currently works when using the web app from a browser, such as Chrome.

Use the My Maps link to access: **mymaps.google.com**.

Additional support with My Maps can be found here:

» geotools.co/mapshelp

What You Can Do Tomorrow

Here are ideas of what you can do in your classroom tomorrow using My Maps:

Create a My Map, share with students, ask students to drop a marker on a location, and have them respond to a writing prompt within their marker.

Have students create a My Map, ask them to use the drawing tool to draw two shapes on the map, and ask them to compare the area and perimeter.

Create a My Map and import a data set to analyze.

More suggested ideas for student use and examples with My Maps can be found at geotools.co/exmaps.

"Education is the most powerful weapon which you can use to change the world."

—Nelson Mandela

CHAPTER 2:
See the World with Google Maps

Ms. Jones is a fourth-grade teacher in California. As part of a unit in California history, her students learned about the California missions. Ms. Jones hoped to help her students gain more background knowledge of the missions, including their locations and what they look like today compared to the late 1700s and 1800s. She assigned three missions to each pair of students to make some observations and ask questions (on a graphic organizer she shared via Google Classroom).

Knowing it wouldn't be possible for each student to travel to each mission in person, she decided to use Google Maps to bring the experience to her students. She introduced Google Maps to her students and showed them how to search for their mission locations. She also let them know about the tools on the map that would let them explore and look around the missions as if they were standing right there. She didn't tell them exactly how to do this; instead, she let them explore and waited to see what they discovered. Her ultimate goal was for her students to find Earth View and Street View in Google Maps to transport them right to the missions.

As the students found Street View imagery and navigated the 3D views on Google Maps, their excitement grew. They became intrinsically motivated to find out about the world and how they relate to these historical locations. By increasing students' curiosities of the world in which they live, we increase their desire to care for and respect it.

GOOGLE MAPS: An Overview

During Google's opening keynote at Google I/O 2016, CEO Sundar Pichai mentioned Google wants to connect individuals with people, places, and things. For us, Google Maps immediately came to mind as a resource that does exactly that. Google Maps is one of our favorite go-to apps!

Google Maps launched in 2005 as a tool to help people find locations and get driving directions. That's how most people still use it today, but its features have evolved well beyond those common tasks. Google Maps is primarily a "consumer" site (with some customization features for the user), whereas My Maps is a "creator" site. The two work together, and Google developers are continually improving the integration between My Maps and Google Maps. Let's explore the opportunities (and possibilities) for using Google Maps in the classroom—or anywhere!

Three Ways to Access Google Maps

> » Go to the website: maps.google.com.
> » Download it as an Android or iOS app from Google Play or the App Store.
> » Click on the Launchpad (or waffle icon) in the top right corner of a Google search page.

When the web page opens, your students are brought into a map with a white Search Google Maps bar. If your students have allowed Google to use their location, the map will display a blue dot showing where they currently are.

Search and Explore

Your students can use Google Maps to visit anywhere in the world. Start by having them search for and explore a location. In the Search Google Maps bar, type in a location to find. This can be a place, type of place (e.g., coffee shops), cities, countries, addresses, coordinates, etc. As your students type, Google will try to predict what they are looking for by listing suggested terms below the search box. If they click on one of those suggestions, the results will populate on the map, some even with the icon of the type of location (e.g., coffee cup for coffee shops). Beneath the search bar, a list of the places shown on the map will appear along with a few options to narrow search results such as price, rating, and hours.

PRO TIP: Students can use their cursor to change the scope of the map. The searched locations will update if the box at the bottom of the search result list is checked to update results when the map moves.

If students hover over a location in the search results, a marker will appear on the map pointing to that specific location. Clicking on a location in the search results list will open an info card with additional details about that location (hours of operation, website, address, and options to save the location, share it, or see what's nearby). Students can use this to learn more about a location in a variety of ways:

» Read the quick facts.

» Check out the reviews.

» See when the business is busiest.

» Explore images and upload their own as a public contribution.

» Click on the location website (if listed) to learn more.

» Add a label. (Label the places you frequent the most.)

» Save it as a location on their Google Maps. (Click on the Star.)

» Search nearby.

» Send the location to their phone if using a desktop computer and mobile device.

» Share the location (via link) or Embed it into a website.

PRO TIP: Labeling and saving locations to a list are a great way to reference locations that one needs to find quickly. As a teacher, if you are needing to plan a lesson you can label locations or save locations to a list. The labeled locations and lists are saved in Your places which is found in the Maps menu.

For students, if they are planning a presentation or virtual tour, they can create saved lists of locations for easy reference (FIGURE 2.1).

FIGURE 2.1

Get Directions

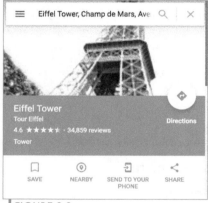

FIGURE 2.2

From the info card, it is also possible to look up directions from one location to another. Clicking on the Directions icon (FIGURE 2.2) will open an option for students to type in *to* and *from* destinations. The location selected from the search result list will automatically populate as the destination, and the starting point will be left open for students to type in another location (e.g., their current location or another nearby location). They can also reverse the directions by clicking on the arrows icon (FIGURE 2.3) to the right of the to/from locations.

Students can also select different modes of transportation (FIGURE 2.4) for the directions. Google Maps will start with suggestions for the recommended mode of transportation, with the option to switch it to one of the following:

» Driving

» Public Transportation

» Walking

» Cycling

» Flights/Flying

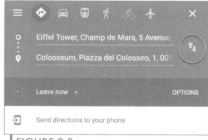

FIGURE 2.3

This is an opportunity for students to do some comparing of modes of transportation and how long each one takes to get to or from specific locations. For further ideas on how to incorporate this into a lesson, please see geotools.co/trasnport.

FIGURE 2.4

Marker Features

Another option with a location/marker on the map is to **right**-click on the marker. This also brings up some additional and useful options:

» Directions to or from the location

» What's here? (Clicking this will open a box that shows the latitude and longitude of that marker.)

» Search nearby

» Print

» Add a missing place

» Report a data problem

» Measure Distance—we love this feature. Once activated, students can click elsewhere on the map to draw lines measuring the distance from that location. Each time your students click, the line will extend, and a white dot will appear. The dots can be dragged to alter the path, or they can be removed by clicking on them. At the bottom of the map, an info card will display the distance measured. Click the X in the top right corner of the info card to close it.

PRO TIP: Need to find the LATITUDE and LONGITUDE of a location? By right-clicking on ANY location (with or without a marker) in Google Maps and clicking "What's Here?" in the context menu, you get the exact latitude and longitude of that spot. Great for when you want to set up geocaching or other navigation-related activities!

Earth View

The Google Earth experience is now part of Google Maps. An option in the bottom left corner of Google Maps allows students to switch to **Satellite view**. In this view they can see satellite imagery and virtually visit the area using navigation options that appear in the bottom right corner. Satellite view allows a user to explore an area by zooming in and out, tilting the view, and even getting a close-up street-level view:

» Zooming *all the way out* brings your students into the view of a globe with real-time weather. They can use the mouse to move the earth around. This view allows them to rotate the earth to see day (along with the sun) and night (in real time to your location).

» Zoom *all the way out* to find options for outer space. Once you are zoomed out, you have the options to explore Mercury, Venus, Mars, the International Space station, earth's moon, and more (FIGURE 2.5)!

» Zooming in allows students to explore a location in greater detail (in both 2D and 3D views). They can see a city layout, find their own homes or school, find buildings and landmarks, view landscapes, etc. Click on the 2D or 3D above the +/- zooming tools to toggle between the two views.

FIGURE 2.5

FIGURE 2.6

» To further explore in either view, use the rotate/tilt tools (FIGURE 2.6) to rotate/orient the globe. Zoom in to see a 3D view of a location/building/street, etc.

» Holding down the ctrl (control) key while dragging on the map will allow navigation around the different views and perspectives of the 3D interface. Give this a try in any city that has large buildings (New York, San Francisco, Chicago, etc.).

» Right-clicking on a location and clicking Measure Distance will let you measure distances and routes from one location to another.

PRO TIP: At any time on the map it is possible to hide (collapse) the side panel on the left. Up at the top next to the search bar there is a tiny grey triangle. Clicking this will open and close the info panel (FIGURE 2.7).

FIGURE 2.7

PRO TIP: Satellite view in Google Maps can be bandwidth heavy, meaning it can take some time—depending on the device and internet connection—to load all the detailed features.

Explore Bar

FIGURE 2.8

The Explore Bar feature in Google Maps takes exploration of a location to the next level. To open the Explore bar, click on the two upward facing arrows beneath the +/- zoom tools (FIGURE 2.8).

In the Explore bar, students will see imagery of the location they're viewing. Hovering the cursor over an image will cause a line to appear that points to the location on the map where the image was taken.

Click on an image in the Explore bar to enlarge it. When opened, click and drag with a mouse to see the entire image. The images here in

Google Maps are user created, which means students can take pictures as well as 360° images and share them on Google Maps as Street View. You'll learn more about 360° images and uploading user-created content in the next chapter.

PRO TIP: If you are having trouble getting the Explore Bar to show up, make sure you (or your students) do not have an active specific location search; for instance, if you search Eiffel Tower, once you are there you can clear the search by clicking on

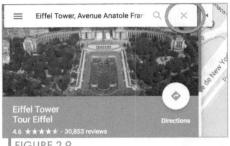

FIGURE 2.9

the X in the search bar. At this point, the Explore Bar shows up and you can explore the area around the Eiffel Tower (FIGURE 2.9).

Pegman

FIGURE 2.10

To the left of the Explore bar is an icon that looks like a person (FIGURE 2.10). This is Pegman. Pegman allows us to step into an immersive imagery experience right in Google Maps, known as Street View. Street View launched almost ten years ago, and the Street View vehicles have been driving around ever since, capturing scenes from cities, towns, and rural areas. You may even see it in your area. The cameras on top of the vehicle and maps decorating the outside of the car are a dead giveaway (FIGURE 2.11).

Street View is an amazing way for students to feel as if they are at a location—even if it is hundreds or thousands of miles away. To launch into Street View, click on Pegman. The roads will turn blue where Street View imagery is available. Blue dots on the map indicate places where

FIGURE 2.11

360° images are available, and orange dots denote where imagery is available to see inside a location. (A key at the bottom of the map will also appear, detailing these colors.) To visit any of the content, students need to simply click on any of the blue dots or lines and watch as the map zooms to a street-level view.

When navigating and exploring in Street View, it is easy to jump to another nearby place on the map by clicking on a new location in the Street View box at the bottom left of the screen (FIGURE 2.12). By bringing up the Explore Bar, your students can also travel through an area by choosing an image with circular arrow icon beside the image title. Click on that image to show Street View. Your students can travel down the same path as the Street View car by using the circle with an arrow inside the image. Each time you click on that circle, Street View zooms down the street to a new location.

FIGURE 2.12

Navigate Through Time

FIGURE 2.13

The Street View images also allow students to explore past imagery collections (in some locations, images are available as far back as 2007). To use this feature, click on a blue line from the Street View map. When the image zooms into view, you'll notice a clock icon in the upper left corner under the location name. Click the clock and a historical imagery bar will appear, showing the years when other photos are available (FIGURE 2.13).

Using Street View History in the Classroom

By using the historical imagery option, teachers can provide an opportunity for students to see how much a location has changed (or hasn't changed) over a relatively small period. There are great opportunities here to foster inquiry and question students about a location (e.g., Why did it change? What was here before? How did it change? What was happening in our community that might have caused it to change? Could we have prevented it from changing? etc.).

For example, Ms. Weisser was teaching a unit on natural disasters that impact the earth. She wanted her students to explore immersive imagery that shows an example of these changes. Using Street View and historical imagery, she was able to have her students look at the before and after of some of the most affected areas in Japan from the 2011 earthquake and tsunami, allowing them to make discoveries, ask questions, and think critically about how natural disasters cause change.

Sharing Images from Google Maps

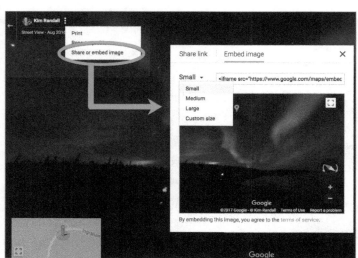

FIGURE 2.14

Once the view is set to the "perfect" view, it is possible to share and/or embed that into a website. To do this, click on the three-dot menu in the upper left next to the location and marker icon (FIGURE 2.14). One of the available options is Share or embed image. Click on that option and then copy the embed code provided. The code can then be pasted into a webpage editor, such as Google Sites (FIGURE 2.15).

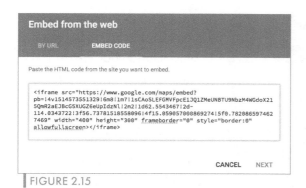

FIGURE 2.15

We'll explore Street View in more depth in Chapter 3, including Street View treks, mobile apps, and creating with Street View.

Additional Google Maps Features

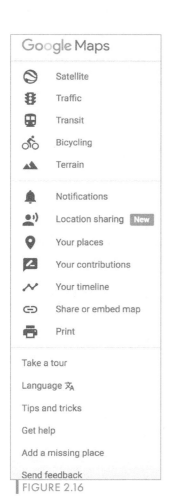

FIGURE 2.16

To reveal even more options in Google Maps, click on the three-bar menu icon to the left of the search bar. (In our classrooms, we refer to this menu as the "stacked hamburger." The reference makes it easy for students to recognize the icon.) In Google Maps, this menu reveals a number of features. The first section of this menu offers the following views:

- » **Satellite**—This switches from Map view to Satellite view.
- » **Traffic**—This shows Live traffic as well as Typical traffic for specific times of day. (This feature is one of our favorites!)
- » **Transit**—This shows public transportation routes.
- » **Bicycling**—This displays dedicated bike trails, lanes, bike-friendly roads, and dirt/unpaved roads.
- » **Terrain**—This shows the topography of the area.

The second section in this menu list is all about personalizing content (FIGURE 2.16):

- » **Notifications**—This is for sharing images of locations visited.
- » **Location sharing**—Others can share their location on the map and mobile app.

FIGURE 2.17

» **Your places**—These are your saved locations, labeled places, and your custom maps from My Maps, which can open in Google Maps (FIGURE 2.17) and be seen in Earth View as well.

» **Your contributions**—This shows any photos or 360° images you've uploaded and shared to Google Maps.

» **Your timeline**—This launches into a page that shows a timeline of locations visited. This uses the student's location history from their phones, so make sure that is on too. The timeline is searchable by year, month, and date.

» **Share or embed map**—This provides a link to share or an embed code that can be added to a blog or webpage.

» **Print**

The third and fourth sections provide features to enhance user experience on Google Maps.

» **Take a tour**—This offers a guided interactive tour of Google Maps (highly recommended).

» **Language**—This allows users to change the language of Google Maps, tools, and menus.

» **Tips and tricks**—This provides quick tips for making the most of Google Maps.

» **Get help**—This allows users to search the Google Maps help forum.

» **Adding a missing place**—This empowers users to update Google Maps.

» **Send feedback**—This provides an outlet if there are additional feature suggestions for Google Maps.

» **Search settings**—This allows you to change settings, such as Safe-Search, search results shown per page, privacy, etc.

» **History**—This shows your Google Drive and Google Chrome activity history.

Google Maps Support and Help Page

For more information or help using specific features, visit:

» support.google.com/maps

Extension Activities with Google Maps

Web developers and geo enthusiasts have used the Google Maps API code and capabilities to form a variety of interactive and immersive experiences.

Please see our site geotools.co/moremaps for direct links to the following projects:

Gallery of Google Maps

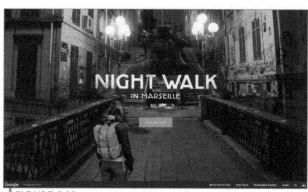

FIGURE 2.18

» **Google Maps Gallery**—Google Maps with Data

» **Google Night Walk**—Explore great cities at night (FIGURE 2.18)

» **World Wonders**—Google Cultural Institute

» **Google Art Project**—Art, Galleries, and Museums in Street View

» **Yad Vashem**—Remembering the Holocaust

» **Dead Sea Scrolls**—Digitizing Biblical manuscripts

» **Nelson Mandela Centre of Memory**—Presenting Nelson Mandela's legacy online

» **Google Street Art**—Street Art mapped and archived

- » **Instant Street View**
- » **Street View Collection**—Google Maps
- » **Colleges with Street View**
- » **ShowMyStreet**— Visit your house
- » **Behind the Scenes**—With Google Maps Street View [video]
- » **Report a Problem**—A collection of art based on Google Street View glitches

Fun and Games with Google Maps

FIGURE 2.19

- » **SmartyPins**—Trivia in Google Maps
- » **GeoGuessr**—Let's Explore the World!
- » **The Secret Door**—Drop into new places in Street View (FIGURE 2.19)!
- » **Build with Chrome**—Google Maps with Legos!
- » **Google Maps**—Pokémon Challenge
- » **8-Bit Google Maps**
- » **Into the Wild map**
- » **Book Thief map**
- » **Harry Potter's Diagon Alley**
- » **QuizUp**—Google Maps Challenges for your Android and iPhone
- » **Teleporter**—Instant teleportation to random places around the world

- » **Johnny Cash has been Everywhere (explicit)**—The song animated on a map
- » **NYC and LA Music Map**—Pinpoints the city's greatest song references—(Source)
- » **API Demos**—More than a map
- » **Pegman Live**—All the artistic versions of the beloved Pegman

Tools and Educational Content

» **Google Sightmap**—A heat map showing the most-photographed locations in the world

» **API Demos**—More than a Map

» **PlanIt! for Photographers (Android App)**—All-in-one solution that is designed to leverage the map and simulated viewfinder technologies (VR, AR etc.) to provide the necessary tools for photographers to pre-visualize the scene in combination with the Sun, Moon, Stars, and Milky Way

» **Maps Timeline**

» **Indoor Maps**—Map your school or other building for others to explore

» **Your Google Map History**—See all the places you've been on Google Maps with Google Location History

» **My Reading Mapped (blog)**

» **Go Back in Time with Google Streetview (no DeLorean required!)**

» **Moon and Mars**—Visit them on Google Maps (watch the video demo)

» **BBC Dimensions**—How Big, Really?

» **Google Crisis Map**

» **Josh Williams' site:** geteach.com/maps/

» **Map your Distance:** mappedometer.com

Staying Safe Using the Companion App

It is especially important to help graduating seniors stay safe and connected as they head off to college, careers, and more. The Companion mobile app for Android and iOS works with Google Maps technology. This app allows an individual user to notify a selected group of people when they are traveling in an unfamiliar area of a city or simply walking back home alone. The selected friends (or parents) can then track the user's progress. Another communication tool in the app lets the user easily communicate with the police if there is a problem. With the click of a button, someone's contact list and/or the authorities can be notified of an issue, and help can be on the way. For more information on this app, visit geotools.co/companion.

What You Can Do Tomorrow

Here are ideas of what you can do in your classroom tomorrow using Google Maps:

» Search for a location, switch into 3D earth view, and use as a writing prompt (FIGURE 2.20).

» Use directions to compute distances and travel time between several locations.

» Have student search for locations to find the latitude/longitude.

» Using the elevation feature compute how long it would take to hike/walk up an elevated location.

FIGURE 2.20

"You cannot get through a single day without having an impact on the world around you. What you do makes a difference, and you have to decide what kind of difference you want to make."

—Jane Goodall

CHAPTER 3:
Create an Immersive Learning Experience with Global Imagery

Have you ever wished you could magically transport your learners to another geographic location? Maybe you thought if you could just take your students to a specific location, they would better understand the setting for a novel, or the impact of an environment on a battle, or even just a foreign landscape in its entirety.

Mr. Sundstrum teaches eleventh-grade English, and while his class was reading *A Thousand Splendid Suns*, it occurred to him that his students may not completely be able to grasp the setting of the novel: environmental extremities, distances between cities, and changes from one place to another. Afghanistan and Pakistan, as well as the journey between, needed to be seen and not just read about by the students in his class.

By using Street View, Mr. Sundstrum took his students on a virtual field trip to explore images from the cities mentioned in the novel. The 360° images allowed students to immerse themselves directly into Herat, Kabul, and Murree, wherein they could navigate the scenes and travels described in the book. Mr. Sundstrum guided their experience by posing big-thinking questions and then giving the students time to explore and reflect. His kids were able to draw connections between book and world, book and self, and ultimately, world and self.

Street View will get your students looking at the world through an immersive lens rather than a flat picture. Many students are already familiar with Google Maps; Street View imagery allows them to interact with this tool in a new way.

In the previous chapter, we touched on a few ways you can use Google Maps and Street View in your classroom. In this chapter, we'll explore even more ways you can use this immersive technology to enhance your students' learning experiences.

Getting a Bigger Picture with STREET VIEW

The Google Maps team has traveled across seven continents—more than sixty-five countries and seven million miles—to create a wealth of 360° imagery. Not only has the Google Maps team taken millions of photos around the globe, but now with the Street View app, any user can take 360° images and upload them to the gallery. With the capability of public contribution, the gallery of imagery has grown exponentially. You can access Street View imagery through Google Maps or the Street View app.

What is a 360° Image?

A 360° image is a single file comprised of several images that have been seamlessly stitched together. This 360° view provides students the virtual experience of being in a location.

Using the arrow icons that appear on the 360° images, students can look up, down, left, and right (FIGURE 3.1). From the ground below to the sky above, every detail is captured in these images.

FIGURE 3.1

Using Street View on a Computer

You can bypass using Google Maps and go right into Street View using the Street View site at google.com/streetview. The Street View site allows you to peruse Google's curated collections of images for famous locations and landmarks.

> » As a reminder, if you want to explore Street View imagery from any place in the world, you will need to start in Google Maps and then use Pegman for exploration of Street View content.

Using the Street View Mobile App

Many students have mobile devices (smartphones and/or tablets). While rules about using these devices in the classroom vary from school to school, we believe it makes sense to incorporate the use of this powerful technology in our lessons. If we know kids are carrying devices that can access the world's information, it is our responsibility to foster their skills for using technology appropriately. Because the Street View mobile app allows users to not only consume but also create and publish content, teachers can give students the opportunity to create and contribute to the global community by sharing their own 360° images.

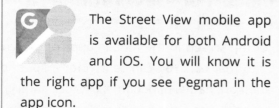

Share Your Own 360° Images

The Street View mobile app is available for both Android and iOS. You will know it is the right app if you see Pegman in the app icon.

The first time you open the app, you will want to give permission for it to access your photos and camera. By allowing Photos access, you are then able to open 360° images from your camera in the Street View app. By allowing Camera access, you are then able to take your own 360° images and publish them to the Google gallery of 360° images.

Overview of Google Street View App

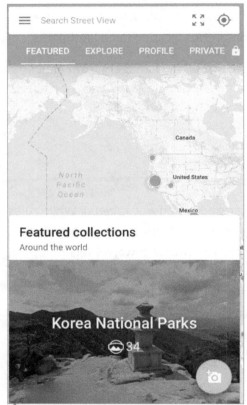

FIGURE 3.2

» **Three-bar menu**—This opens the account sign-in/profile settings as well as tips, gallery, and help menus.

» **Search bar**—Here you can enter a desired location for Street View to find.

» **Navigation bar**—This shows Featured collections, Explore, Profile (your 360° images), Private (photos that you've taken but have not made public), and Contribute (shows nearby locations that need 360° photos.)

» **Results**—Search results or nearby 360° images appear at the bottom of your screen.

» **Map area**—This is the main portion of your screen that shows you a map or photo. Use your fingers to "pinch" the map or image to zoom in and zoom out by spreading your fingers apart. If you zoom into street level, the blue lines and Pegman will appear.

» **Create button**—Indicated by a camera with a plus symbol, this icon leads to options for you to link a 360° camera or to import 360° photos. (FIGURE 3.2)

Searching for 360° Images on the Street View Mobile App

A search bar is located at the top of the screen in the mobile app. To search for images, simply type a location into that bar. You can search for a specific address or a specific place (e.g., a landmark name, park name, city, or country). Once you've entered your search term, the app will navigate to that part of the world and display the search results. Typically, the first results listed for an area are the most popular, but if you zoom in on the map, more results will appear. You can zoom in closer and move the map around to focus on other areas, and more content will keep populating and appearing. (FIGURE 3.2)

Expand Their Worlds

A goal of using geo tools is to foster a global experience that sparks curiosity in your students. After a directed classroom activity, you may find kids want to see their home, or a childhood favorite place, or someplace they have always wanted to know more about. You can create connections between the places you are studying and the places they seek by asking questions or allowing students to share their findings.

Scroll through the results list to find an image you would like to view. Click on that 360° image and open it in your app's main screen. At this point, you have a couple of options for viewing the image. If you click and drag the image, you can manually navigate the 360° view. There are two other interactive options, however:

FIGURE 3.3

» If you click on the VR cardboard symbol (FIGURE 3.3) at the top right (FIGURE 3.4), the image will split in two so you can view it with a Google Cardboard or other virtual reality (VR) viewer (FIGURE 3.5).

» If you click on the compass symbol in the top right, you can navigate the 360° image by moving your mobile device left and right, up and down. You can also pinch or push with two fingers to zoom in and out.

FIGURE 3.4

FIGURE 3.5

Sharing Images from Google Street View App

FIGURE 3.6

To share a 360° image with friends or to post it on your website, click on the share button (FIGURE 3.6). You can then save the image to your mobile device's camera roll, send in a message, or post on social media.

NOTE: The image's metadata goes with the image when it is saved to the camera roll and passed along between viewers. This information includes location and publishing data. If you use a 360° image, make sure you have permission and give credit to the photographer.

A Journey to Global Citizenship

After eighteen years in the elementary classroom, Mr. Pareja decided to switch up a few things while teaching his students about animals, specifically penguins. He took his class on a journey around the globe examining the various penguin habitats (FIGURE 3.7). This ultimately led to a discussion about environmental concerns and endangered animals as well as where in the world to explore next.

We can help our kids grow into global citizens by fostering their curiosity. We as humans are natural learners. As teachers, we can create opportunities for inquiry-based learning, curiosity-led learning, and global exploration.

FIGURE 3.7

Using Street View—and 360° images in particular—allows students to notice things while immersed in a virtual reality. It allows them to pick where to look and foster observational skills. They will notice small details within a setting and discover similarities and differences between the immersive scene and their own reality.

Taking 360° Images Using the Street View App

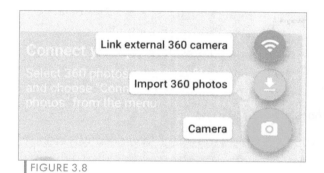

FIGURE 3.8

On the main screen of the mobile app, you'll find an orange icon with a camera and plus symbol. You'll tap this icon to take your own 360° images using your smartphone (FIGURE 3.8). When you click on this option, you'll be prompted to open your camera and allow the app to access it.

Once the camera is opened, you will see a circle in the center of your screen. Raise your device and center the yellow dot within the circle. When the dot and circle are aligned, tap the dot to take a picture of that view. Once you have captured that spot, move your device right or left and repeat the process of centering the dot within the circle and taking the photo.

The circle at the bottom of your screen will show the progress of your captures. Once the progression circle completes itself and your checkmark turns green, you have completed the 360° image. Tap the checkmark to finish the image.

Upon tapping the checkmark, Pegman will become animated and show you that your image is being stitched together. When the process is complete (it may take a few seconds), a confetti celebration will let you know your 360° image is ready. You can tap on the image to open it, navigate, view it with Google Cardboard, and even publish it to the public gallery.

You will want to name the location of the 360° image once it has been stitched together. Under the image, you can click on the location symbol and name the photo.

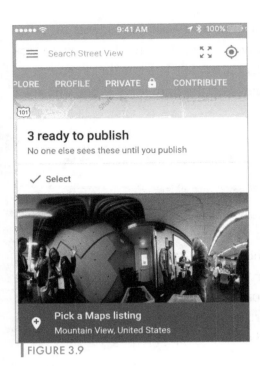

FIGURE 3.9

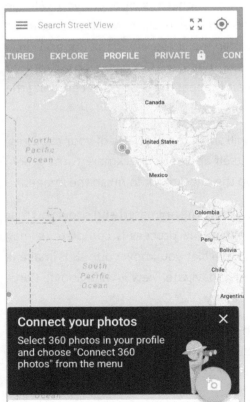

FIGURE 3.10

PRO TIP: The Street View app works with spherical cameras to take 360° images in one click. It is also possible to take 360° images in interval mode (captures images automatically) and connect them together as Street View. Currently, trusted Street View photographers and local guides (level 6 and above) are also able to shoot in video mode and convert it to Street View.

Publishing Options

You can publish the image in various ways (FIGURE 3.9):

1. Tap on Private on the navigation bar. This will show you all the 360° images you've taken but not yet published. From there you can select which 360° images to publish.

2. Tap on the 360° image to select it and then click on the Publish to Google Maps bar located on the top of the 360° image info card.

3. You can now create Google Street View paths and navigation routes with your own mobile device. For more information and tutorials on this, please visit geotools.co/selftrek (FIGURE 3.10).

Sharing 360° Images between Classrooms

One idea for getting students to make observations and use deductive skills is to share 360° images between classrooms. You can save a 360° image to your camera roll by clicking on the Share icon of your 360° image. Once saved to the camera roll, it can be messaged or emailed to another classroom.

When one classroom receives another classroom's image, have the students try to figure out the mystery location. By making observations through viewing the 360° image, students create questions about the scene they are discovering. Using messaging or a Google Hangout, classes can ask questions about the setting. This helps foster inquiry-based learning, as well as collaborative processing and problem solving.

STEM Application: Students could investigate plants and native plant identification by viewing a 360° image of a local park, riverbank, lake area, or forest.

ELA Application: Students could use a Street View scene as part of a writing prompt. Students could be asked to identify concrete details from what they can see while immersed in the scene.

What You Can Do Tomorrow

Here are ideas of what you can do in your classroom tomorrow using Street View:

» Have students search in Google Maps and open up a location in Street View, look around a location, and compare today vs X number of years ago.

» Using the Street View site (google.com/streetview), select a collection for students to explore (direct inquiry) or have students self-select (guided inquiry), and have the students complete a 3-2-1 chart (3 Things I Observe, 2 Things I Think, and 1 Thing I Wonder) as they explore the location.

"Our happiest moments as tourists always seem to come when we stumble upon one thing while in pursuit of something else."

—Lawrence Block

CHAPTER 4:
Exploring Virtual Reality and Creating Multimedia Projects with 360° Images

Ms. Gosser, a seventh-grade teacher, was starting the biome unit with her students. To try to enhance the learning and frontload the unit with an immersive experience, she brought in a virtual reality experience for her students. Using some refurbished mobile devices and virtual reality viewers, the students were taken through a Google Expedition on biomes.

For each biome, the students made an entry on their graphic organizer. Then, before adding any further details to their papers, they explored that biome through virtual reality. They were able to articulate what they were noticing, what natural elements were present or missing, and what similarities and differences each biome had. After a visit to a biome, the students then added details to their graphic organizers.

Ms. Gosser found that her students' retention and understanding of biomes had improved due to the experience through virtual reality.

Special 360° Image Collection: Going Underwater with Google

In September 2012, the XL Catlin Seaview Survey commenced. Its mission is to create a baseline survey of the world's coral reefs so there is better articulation about the destruction, and henceforth needed preservation efforts, of our reefs. More than 150 kilometers of reefs have been documented thus far with over 105,000 high-resolution 360° images taken. The team has captured survey results as deep as 125 meters (FIGURE 4.1).

This survey has created a thorough baseline of the world's coral reefs, and our students can benefit from these images—both in seeing the beauty of the reefs and in seeing a need to preserve them. While the site is rich with imagery, it also hosts a wide array of information and analysis of the research.

To learn more, go to geotools.co/underwater.

FIGURE 4.1

Immersive Tours

FIGURE 4.2

The Google Maps team has traveled the Earth, capturing some of its finest geographic gems. Called Trekkers, the individuals who seek to map the earth where cars cannot go can be found walking, hiking, diving, boating, and/or flying to capture Earth's imagery. For you and your students, you can take immersive tours of places that may be elusive or inaccessible for visitors. For instance, you can hike Mount Everest or see Venice via boat. You can increase students' curiosity by touring remote Cambodian temples, such as Angkor Wat, and walk paths that are no longer open to the public. For links and how to access specific tours, please visit our resource site: geotools.co/gofurther.

Jumping into Virtual Reality with Google Cardboard

Many of us want to bring new experiences to our students, and virtual reality (VR) is a powerful and interactive way to do that. While there are some very expensive VR tools on the market, Google Cardboard's free app, which uses your smartphone and a number of VR devices (ranging from almost free to $40), makes the immersive digital experience available to everyone.

To experience virtual reality, a headset (VR viewer) is necessary. These viewers can be purchased or constructed of cardboard using instructions from the Google Cardboard site: vr.google.com/cardboard. Images or videos viewed using a smartphone, VR viewer, and the Google Cardboard app offer a completely immersive experience wherein users can move around to view new areas of the 360° scene. Some VR videos and images also include sound, motion graphics, and interactive content.

Google Cardboard Tutorial

To use the Cardboard app or any other virtual reality app, you need to have a smartphone and Google Cardboard. Open the Cardboard app and click Launch Cardboard Demos. You will see an animation showing you how to turn your phone and place it in the Cardboard viewer. Once you have the smartphone in the Cardboard viewer and are looking at the app through it, you will see a digital landscape environment along with some menu options:

Google Cardboard for iOS
Or visit geotools.co/iosCBapp

Google Cardboard for Android
Or visit geotools.co/androidCB

For this first experience, go ahead and choose Urban Hike. You can select your choice by hovering the cursor you see within your view over Urban Hike and then clicking the button on the Cardboard viewer. The button is located on the right side of the Cardboard viewer. You will be taken to a famous landmark location. Perhaps you start at the Eiffel Tower.

Look around, turn left and right, up and down. When you are ready to explore the next location, look down toward the ground. You should see some text. Hover over the text and click the button on your Cardboard viewer. Your next destination awaits!

Once you have figured out how to work with Google Cardboard using the Cardboard app, you can branch out. Many other apps offer Cardboard viewing options. Google Street View can be viewed using Cardboard, putting the viewer directly into any 360° image.

For more Google Cardboard apps and resources, visit our website:
» geotools.co/vr

GOOGLE EXPEDITIONS in the Classroom

While being able to explore virtual reality with one headset is nice, educators asked for a better option. There was a need to be able to bring virtual reality to the classroom. At Google I/O in 2015, Google announced they were creating a classroom platform wherein an entire classroom could participate in a Google Cardboard virtual reality experience as a class, with multiple headsets functioning at one time. The Google Expeditions kit became available in the fall of 2015. By mid-2016, over one million students had taken virtual field trips through the Google Expeditions app. As of July 2017, Google has released a standalone version of the app so that even a single person can enjoy the content without having to have a guide present.

How Google Expeditions Works

The Google Expeditions kit contains mobile devices and VR headsets for each student, a router, and a teacher device for guiding the expedition. Each device needs to have the Google Expeditions app installed on it. Prior to the lesson, the teacher device will have connected to the internet and downloaded the Expedition content. On the day of the Google Expeditions lesson, students and the instructor need to connect to the same network signal using the kit's router.

NOTE: you do not need to be on your school's network or have internet during the expedition.

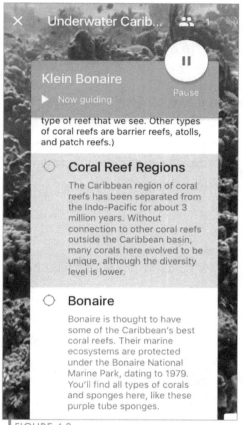

FIGURE 4.3

Because the content is already downloaded to the instructor's device, the teacher is going to be sending the content through the router to the student's headsets. The teacher controls what the students are seeing through the viewers (FIGURE 4.3).

As a teacher, you will want to find the Google Expedition content you would like to use with your students prior to that day's lesson. Before you can lead, you will need to download the expeditions you would like to use to your device.

PRO TIP: Your students will need to take breaks while viewing content in a VR viewer. Make sure to give direct instructions for when to lift the headsets to their faces, when you are about to shift to another scene, and when to put down the headsets for discussion, processing, and reflection.

Once the students are connected, have the app open, and are following you as the guide, you can engage them in any of the downloaded Expeditions. Click on an expedition to load it. To send it to your students' devices, hit the Play button. Students will then be sent the immersive imagery that you see on your own device. You, as the instructor, can also see content as well as inquiry questions. You can shift between scenes and send them to the students' viewers.

Within a scene, you can draw attention to various points of interest. You can either click on the compass icons pre-determined and provided for you on the info card, or you can click and hold on the screen to create your own point of interest. Students will be directed to follow arrows until they are all looking at your selected point of interest.

Google Expeditions allows teachers to take students to destinations all over the world, within the human body, and throughout places in spaces. You can explore historical artifacts as well. Through this kit, a teacher can put students into an immersive experience that allows for them to interact with a place instead of view it flat within a textbook.

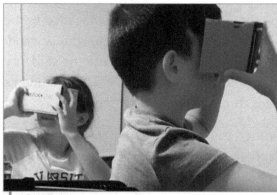

FIGURE 4.4

To learn more about Google Expeditions (FIG-URE 4.4) and how to create your own home-grown Expedition kit (as well as see a list of all the possible Expeditions), please visit geotools.co/expeditions.

 # Creating Interactive Experiences with Story Spheres

A Story Sphere is a 360° image that contains audio files. When a viewer is immersed in a Story Sphere 360° image, they can hover the cursor dot over an audio icon and the audio file will begin to play. This functionality allows creators to enhance 360° images with interactive narration.

You can use your Google account to sign in at StorySpheres.com and create an interactive 360° image. Since this is a browser-based creation tool, you or your students can create a Story Sphere from a mobile device or desktop computer (FIGURE 4.5).

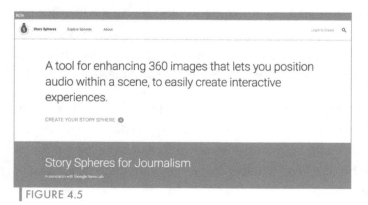

FIGURE 4.5

To prepare for the project, you will first need to gather the project files (or assets). At a bare minimum, you will need one 360° image and one MP3 audio file. Save these in a location where you can access them so they are ready to upload to the Story Sphere website.

FIGURE 4.6

Once you are signed into Story Spheres, click on Create (FIGURE 4.6) and give your project a title. From there you will work through three main steps to publish your Story Sphere for others to view: Upload, Studio and Share (FIGURE 4.7).

NOTE: We have posted sample files on our website from which you can practice building a Story Sphere. Currently, Story Spheres have a 15 mb file size limit (including image and audio). You can grab the sample 360° images and audio files and follow the directions below to get an idea of the project workflow. Please visit: geotools.co/createss.

FIGURE 4.7

Upload

Once you have given your project a title, you will be taken to the Upload screen. This is where you will upload all your project files. Upload your 360° image and any audio files you want to go with your project, then click Next.

Studio

After uploading your project files, you are taken to the Studio stage for editing and finessing how the files work together. At this point you will see your image along with a flyout menu bar to the right of the screen. Each sound/audio file is color coded to where the icon is on the photo. To move audio icons around in your photo, you will need to adjust the vertical, horizontal, and depth sliders in the right panel (FIGURE 4.7).

Once the audio files are where you want them in your 360° image and you've adjusted the audio level(s) to your liking, you are ready to publish your Story Sphere.

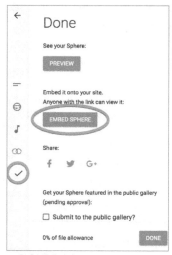

FIGURE 4.8

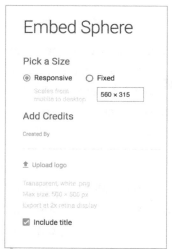

FIGURE 4.9

Share

All your Story Sphere projects are stored under your account on the Story Sphere website. To edit or revise projects, simply log in and navigate to the top of the page. Click My Story Spheres (FIGURE 4.6). Your Story Spheres will appear and can be opened to edit.

Story Spheres can be shared with a link or embedded into web pages, such as Google Sites. This allows for a Story Sphere to be interacted with right on a student web page as part of a project or student portfolio. To find the embed code, open up an existing Story Sphere project using the edit pencil icon. This opens the details page of the project. Click on the checkmark (fifth option down on the left-hand side) (FIGURE 4.8). Next a window opens with the option to preview or embed the Story Sphere (FIGURE 4.8). Select embed sphere, another window opens and options appear (FIGURE 4.9). Scroll to the bottom of the window to the Link option. Copy the link (embed code) (FIGURE 4.10).

FIGURE 4.10

Embedding into Google Sites

FIGURE 4.11

FIGURE 4.12

Open Google Sites, select Embed in the Sites menu and paste the embed code (FIGURE 4.11). A preview will appear (FIGURE 4.12). Click insert and the story sphere will be placed into the Google Site (FIGURE 4.13). When finished adjusting the size and placement, don't forget to click publish in Google Sites to view the site with the new Story Sphere.

FIGURE 4.13

PRO TIP: By embedding story spheres into a central location, such as a Google Site, students are able to easily share and explore one another's projects without having to worry about sending and receiving several links and opening multiple windows.

App Smashing to Create 360° Content

Once you are familiar with taking 360° images and how to view them with VR viewers, you may want to consider other VR creation tools. There are more apps and options developing all the time. To learn more about these tools and possible uses in the classroom, please see geotools.co/createvr.

"A mind that is stretched by a new experience can never go back to its old dimensions."

—Oliver Wendell Holmes

Ideas for Using Story Spheres in the Classroom

» Create 360° images of school locations and publish a virtual tour of the school.

» Add voice narration to a 360° image to create an immersive personal narrative.

» Create a Story Sphere as a teaching tool wherein the audio clips ask students to notice certain things about what they are viewing in the 360° image.

» Create a shared folder of 360° images which students can choose from to use in their Story Sphere projects. Ask them to narrate extended metaphor comparisons to the environment, cultures, politics, world events, and/or personalities.

» Have students create a scene using costumes and capture it in a 360° image. Then they can use Story Spheres to add explanations, dialogue, monologues, and/or narrations.

What You Can Do Tomorrow

Here are ideas of what you can do in your classroom tomorrow using virtual reality:

» Show students in the Street View app how to search, find, and turn locations into imagery they can view in Google Cardboard.

» Show students how they can create their own 360° image with the Street View app, then practice taking photos in the classroom, school, and outside.

» Challenge students to find a location in their community that doesn't have Street View to create their own image.

CHAPTER 5:
Creating a Narrative Using Maps and Tour Builder

Ms. Keck wanted her students to be able to visually demonstrate their understanding of westward expansion. She also wanted to empower them to integrate elements into their presentations that personally appealed to them.

Using Tour Builder, her students created interactive map experiences for their audiences. Not only did each student put together a sequence of locations that showed the American westward expansion routes, they also added pictures and videos reflecting certain aspects of the journey. Through narrative writing, they told the stories of early American pioneers from a variety of angles, weaving in historical data and rich descriptive imagery.

The final presentation of the information was not a sit-and-listen experience where the entire class listens to one student at a time; rather, each student had a station with their tour playing through Google Earth. The students then were able to move from station to station commonly known as gallery walk, watching, reading, and listening to each tour. The students interacted with and gave feedback on one another's tours while learning various aspects of westward expansion.

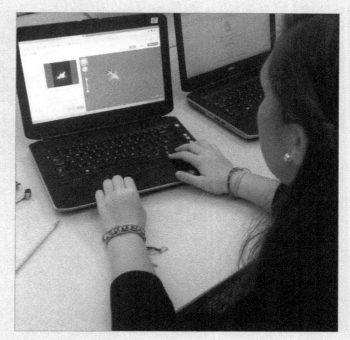

TOUR BUILDER: An Overview

Tour Builder was originally created with military veterans in mind. Google wanted a place for military men and women to document their tours and share insights about where they were stationed. The documenting tool was so successful, Google decided to launch it to the world.

With the power of storytelling at its core, Google Tour Builder provides a way for someone to create a virtual tour of different geographic landmarks and regions. A user can create an experience for an audience in sequential format with smooth-motion transitions. While still in its beta phase, Tour Builder comes with an array of media and text functionality, as well as ways to share a tour publicly or privately.

To access Tour Builder, go to tourbuilder.withgoogle.com and sign in with your Google account. Once you have signed in, you'll have access to the creative tools and your own tour gallery. You will see four navigation options at the top: My Tours, Shared Tours, Gallery, and About (FIGURE 5.1)

FIGURE 5.1

My Tours—All your own created tours will be kept in this section. If you start a tour and need to come back to it later, this is where you'll come to continue your work. If you have not created anything yet, this area will be empty.

Shared Tours—If someone shares a tour with you directly, you will be able to see it here. If no one has directly shared a tour with you, this area won't have any content.

Gallery—Tours that have been published publicly may become part of the gallery rotation of sample tours. The gallery is a library of public tours. Anyone has access to these.

PRO TIP: When having students create tours, send them to the Gallery FIRST. The Gallery has so many great tours from which students can glean inspiration and know-how to level-up their own project planning.

About—The About page is a page where your students can find out more details about Tour Builder. The FAQ is found here and provides details on browser compatibility as well as other important information.

Creating a Tour

To begin creating a tour, click on the red Create New Tour button.

You will be asked to name your project and provide the author's name(s).

Notice the fine print under the name and author fields: "Your tour is completely private until you decide to share it with others." Your tour is not publicly viewable until you decide it's ready. This allows you to view and edit prior to the final publishing.

Navigating the Main Interface

There are three parts to the Tour Builder Project Interface: Left-side Card Navigation, Content Panel, and Map View. Every project also begins with an Introduction card (FIGURE 5.2).

Left-side Card Navigation—On the left side of the screen, you will see a column where the locations on your tour will be laid out like index cards. This allows for organizing the locations as well as providing a way for viewers to jump around between locations. You can always tell which card you are editing or viewing because the text in the selected card is red, while the others are blue.

PRO TIP: You can reorder the locations simply by clicking and dragging a location to a different part of the card order.

Introduction Card—When you open a project, the first card in the Navigation is the Introduction card. This is also where viewers will begin your tour. The map view on the Introduction card will be an overall map showing the complete view of all locations within your tour.

FIGURE 5.2

The Introduction content should give your audience an overview of your tour. You can add an introduction picture by clicking on the Add a Photo button. While you can add several photos per location, you may only add one Introduction photo.

In the text area, you can type or paste in your Introduction text. Use this space to explain your tour, preface your narrative, or pose a problem for your audience to solve while exploring the locations. It should give your audience a good idea of the *why* behind the tour project.

Below the text box, you will choose the type of story, wherein there are five choices. Each option allows for different views and transitions between locations. Depending on which browser you are using, these may appear differently. To view any of the 3D imagery and/or transition patterns, you will need to you will need to open the tour using the new Google Earth. The fifth option—the Disabled option—means that paths are turned off, and you'll simply see the world with location markers, but without travel paths. The default story type is Story 3D.

Below story type, you get to choose your path color. Depending on the purpose or theme of your tour, the color may need to be changed to fit the message going to your audience (FIGURE 5.3).

Once you have the Introduction done, it's time to add a location.

FIGURE 5.3

Add a Location—To add a location to your tour, simply click on the + Add Location button located in the Card Navigation panel. A new location panel will open where you can search for your location and add it to the map, or you can simply drop a marker anywhere on the map.

To drop a marker, click Drop Placemark, a Click to Drop sign will appear letting you know to click anywhere on the map to drop a place marker. You can always give any of your locations a custom name in their content panel.

Content Panel—When you click on a Location card, its content and map view will appear. The Content Panel stores information about the location as well as any added pictures and video.

Very much like the Introduction card, the Content Panel allows you to change the title of the location, add in media and text, and then adjust the icon to best fit the location. To add photos and videos, click inside the Add Photos and Videos box.

You have a variety of options for adding photos and video:

1. Add them from your own Google Drive or YouTube channel.

2. Search the web and add them directly from the search.

3. Upload photos and video from your local computer.

4. Add photos and video hosted on a website by providing the URL for the photo or video.

You can use jpeg, bmp, png, and gif files. You will want to host your videos on YouTube and select them from the YouTube option. Once a photo or video is placed in the box, you can add more using the plus symbol (+) located in the photo box.

PRO TIP: If you choose to include an animated gif in your image gallery, it will only show the animation when you click to view the image full screen.

Classroom Applications for Tour Builder

Instructional ideas for using location cards:

» Put locations in order of events (i.e. historical or chronological perspective).

» Create a tour of a site that had a natural disaster (e.g., San Francisco Earthquakes).

» Show the transfer of plants or artifacts across the globe or region (i.e. invasive plant migration across regions).

PRO TIP: The flexibility of media uploading is fantastic for the classroom, especially in a one-to-one or BYOD (Bring Your Own Device) environment. Students store media in different locations, so having options for finding and uploading media means fewer work arounds and more time spent on content production.

If you are producing a tour that has timeline start and end times, those can be input as well into each location content area.

There is a text box for the narrative or explanatory text. Text can be formatted using the formatting bar, including lists and style options. If you paste in text and it doesn't look the way it should, you can always clear the formatting using the *Tx* option (FIGURE 5.4).

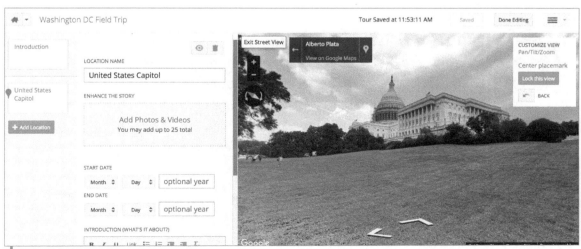

FIGURE 5.4

PRO TIP: Before you allow your students into Tour Builder, have them draft their writing in a Google Doc. This allows them to clearly articulate the verbal portion of their tour before approaching the visual elements. With the writing complete, they only need to copy and paste the text segments into the content panel for each location. This produces a much stronger final project.

For each location card, you can also customize the marker icon. You can choose icons from the library, or you can customize your placemark by using an image file, such as a jpeg, png, bmp, or gif.

NOTE: Animated gifs will not show properly when used for an icon image.

PRO TIP: If you are having students work on tours in small groups, start them in My Maps. Students can work collaboratively on a My Maps and then export that project data as a KML/KMZ file. One group member can then import that data into a Tour Builder project. Since only one person can work on Tour Builder at a time, using My Maps as a collaborative step helps the group stay active and working together. Upon importing the KML/KMZ file into Tour Builder, the group leader can easily tweak the content for final output. Please note ahead of time that you can only add a KML/KMZ file by URL, meaning you will need to host these files somewhere on the web. For more information on how to host files and get direct links to files, go to **geotools.co/directlinks**.

PRO TIP: You have the option for importing KML or KMZ files to your location card. KML stands for keyhole markup language. A KML file can contain mapping data as well as any other information that belongs with a particular map. A KMZ file is a type of .zip file that contains one KML file and possibly other files that have been zipped up together. Remember, you can create KML/KMZ files from My Maps. See page 19.

NOTE: If you import a KMZ file into a specific location card, that data will only be visible when looking at that location card.

Map View

Once you are finished crafting the Content Panel for your location, you will need to set the map view. As a tour author, you can customize the map view for each location in a variety of ways.

The default view for a marker is the map view. Once the location is placed on your tour, you have the option to zoom in or out on map view, go to Street View using Pegman, or use ground-level view. You will want to customize your location view and then click on the Lock This View button. This will freeze that perspective of the location, and your audience will see this when visiting the location through your tour.

There are several ways to navigate around the map view (FIGURE 5.5):

» You can zoom in and out of the map using the + and - symbols.

» There is navigation built into the map as well. Click and drag anywhere on the map to move around.

FIGURE 5.5

» Pegman also allows you to enter Street View. To do this, click and drag Pegman over your map. You can drag and drop him anywhere on the map where there is a blue line indicating Street View imagery is present. When in Street View, you will be able to navigate the scene through the same navigation tools.

» The circle compass lets you rotate around the scene. You can either use your cursor to click and move around the map, or you can click the arrows on the compass to rotate the view 90° either direction.

Viewing a Tour

After your location is fully edited and the map view is set, you are ready to view your tour through your audience's perspective. To exit Editing Mode, click on Done Editing located above the map area. Go ahead and click on the Introduction card and let the project load from the beginning. Now you can preview the entire project as your audience will see it.

Upon loading a tour, you will begin at the Introduction card where you will be able to view the overview map as well as the introductory text and image. From there you can simply click Next and navigate from place to place sequentially. You can also navigate just by clicking on individual location cards. Alternatively, you can view the tour in Full Screen. When you are in Full Screen, the location cards are no longer present, and the Next and Back buttons become your main navigation options for viewing the tour.

PRO TIP: A great way to share tours in class is to have each tour author bring their tour into full-screen viewing mode on a device. Then you can create stations in the room showcasing each tour. Students can gallery walk their way around the classroom, viewing each tour and providing feedback.

Another option to view Tour Builder tours is to open them in the new Google Earth. To do this, click on the menu in the upper right-hand corner (FIGURE 5.6) and select Open in Earth. The first time a tour is opened in Earth, you will need to allow pop-ups in your browser address (FIGURE 5.7). Once allowed, refresh and click Open in Earth again. Your tour will then be launched in new Google Earth (FIGURE 5.8).

FIGURE 5.6

FIGURE 5.7

FIGURE 5.8

PRO TIP: You can make copies of tours. Once a tour is set up the way you'd like, you can then create copies of that tour. For a teacher, this is great if you need to get your students started with a template of a tour. If your students are all studying the journey of a character or historical figure, and each classroom group is responsible for a different perspective of that tour, then it may be beneficial to have a tour template started with the same location points. Then each group can focus more on their own aspects of that journey while staying within a similar reference guideline.

What You Can Do Tomorrow

Here are ideas of what you can do in your classroom tomorrow using Tour Builder:

» Explore existing tours, open one within Tour Builder, choose Open in Earth from the three-bar menu in the upper right corner.

» Preview Tour Builder with your students, and then have them sketch out a plan on paper so when you do have computers for your students, they can spend time producing instead of planning.

» Have students build a tour of concrete locations where specific scientific events have happened.

» Have students use Tour Builder as a storyboard builder, putting locations in order to prepare for writing or explanatory presentations.

"Wherever you go becomes
a part of you somehow."

—Anita Desai

CHAPTER 6:
Creating New Knowledge and Curiosity with Google Earth

Mr. Roanoke wanted to pose a problem to his math students but didn't want to give them the same old worksheet or story problem. He wanted his students to see math as a natural part of their world and for them to see math applications in different aspects of life.

To help his students understand diameter, radius, and circumference, he chose to use Google Earth and posed a variety of challenges related to crop circles. By accessing resources that he had on the web, he created a Hyperdoc lesson and shared it and a specific KMZ file with his students using Google Classroom.

His students then took the KMZ file and uploaded it to their Google Earth accounts. Each student navigated Google Earth from his or her Chromebook, taking time to problem solve the math challenges before them.

GOOGLE EARTH: An Overview

Getting students to explore the world (in person and/or virtually) is vital in helping them realize that we all play an active role in sustaining and maintaining the planet and their collective communities. Google Earth allows just this. On any device, students can use Google Earth to explore monuments, new environments, and historical places.

Google Earth was initially released as a desktop application in 2005. Google Earth superimposes satellite imagery, aerial photography, panoramic and 360° photography, and GIS location systems onto a 3D globe. The app had over one billion downloads as of 2011; however, with the increase in use of Chromebooks in education, it became apparent that Google Earth needed a web version to sustain its audience. With all the app's capabilities, it has required a herculean effort on the part of the Google Geo team to recode Google Earth for the web. As of April 2017, Google Earth now has a web-based version.

Google Earth (2017) is a web app that allows users to visit locations around the globe and interact with knowledge in an immersive location-based format. If a picture tells a thousand words, imagine the impact immersive imagery can have on students. Explorers of all ages can peruse the scenery, follow tours, and even interact with special collections of imagery within Google Earth.

Math in the Real World

If you are interested in the math challenges Mr. Roanoke used with his students, visit realworldmath.org.

If you are looking to find content on the web that you can use with Google Earth, searching for a KML/KMZ file can help.

For History teachers: Try searching "Civil War KML" to find Google Earth content related to the Civil War.

For Science teachers: Try searching "tornadoes KML" to find Google Earth content related to tornadoes.

Now try your own content-specific search!

Accessing Google Earth

To access the web version of Google Earth, visit **earth.google.com/web**.

To install and use the full functionality of the desktop version of Google Earth, please visit **geotools.co/desktopearth** for details

From mapping to embedded images to 3D models, Google Earth can be used to help anyone better understand the context of global events and places. In this section, we will explore how to use Google Earth, not only to view, but also to create and share. The power of Google Earth lies in its creation tools and the ability to build and record sequences of places and media. The beauty of Google Earth lies in its ability to take us to different regions of our planet and tell the story of a place—whether that is its history, its future, or a tale of someone or something living there.

When you land on the new Google Earth webpage, click on launch google earth. Once it loads, a brief tutorial will walk you through the steps of how to search for a place, learn more about that location through info cards, and view locations in 3D. You can also learn how to choose an adventure with Google Earth's Voyager. Here we are going to explore a little deeper into the functionality and uses for Google Earth in the classroom.

In Earth, the main menu is a simple bar on the left (FIGURE 6.1). There are a handful of easy-to-access options, including Search, Voyager, I'm Feeling Lucky, My Places, and Share. There are several differences between the Google Earth desktop app and Google Earth on the web.

FIGURE 6.1

Search

Students will be able to use the search tool when studying different parts of the world. For instance, if students were learning about the differences between urban and rural areas and wanted to visit one of the largest cities in the world, they could search New York City or any part therein. The search results would yield that satellite imagery. The students would be able to understand the geography of the region as well as use Pegman to access the Street View imagery right within Google Earth to visit places like Rockefeller Center (FIGURE 6.2).

FIGURE 6.2

PRO TIP: When you double click on the compass symbol in the bottom right, it pops into the center of the tools and becomes the vertical navigation for the 3D tilt rendering (FIGURE 6.3).

FIGURE 6.3

Voyager

Voyager is built around curated content, some timely (i.e., what is happening with current events or history), and some timeless (i.e., a collection focused on a theme or topic that isn't dependent on a closed timeline). There are themed collections: Editor's Picks, Travel, Nature, Culture, History, and Education. The example given here is for the events that unfolded with Hurricane Irma in September of 2017. Google Newslab teamed up with Google Earth to bring forth imagery of the damage. It included the ability to toggle on or off the recent satellite imagery to see what the land was like before Hurricane Irma (FIGURE 6.4).

FIGURE 6.4

I'm Feeling Lucky

I'm Feeling Lucky is the perfect choice if your students need an activity to spark their curiosity. One way to have students grow their understanding of the earth is to actually travel the earth. When a student clicks the I'm Feeling Lucky menu option, a random place appears in Google Earth. There are information cards that describe the place, and if students so choose, they may explore the area further by clicking on Pegman to enter the Street View imagery found there (FIGURE 6.5).

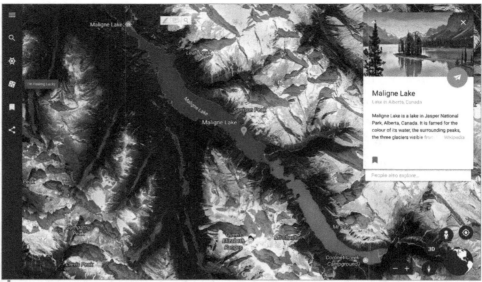

FIGURE 6.5

My Places

The Bookmarks menu option, under the My Places menu, allows users to sign in with their Google account and save locations as Bookmarks. Once you understand how to bookmark content, you can create custom saved location lists. To do this, locate a place in Google Earth that you would like to save. Then click on the Bookmark icon. The location is then added to your list of Bookmarks (FIGURE 6.6).

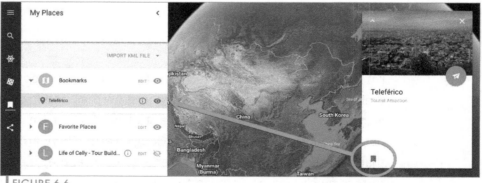

FIGURE 6.6

Once you have a list of locations bookmarked and ready for a lesson, you can save the list of Bookmarks as a custom location list. To do this, open your Bookmark list and find the three-dot menu icon. Choose to duplicate that list (FIGURE 6.7).

Then go into the newly formed list and choose to rename it. Now you have a

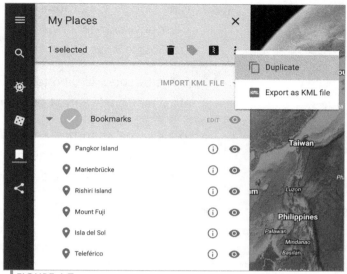

FIGURE 6.7

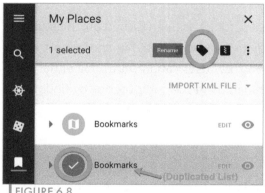

FIGURE 6.8

FIGURE 6.9

custom curated list of locations within Google Earth. You can delete your "Bookmarks" list as it will start fresh the next time you bookmark a location (FIGURE 6.8).

If you were presenting to an entire group, having a custom set of bookmarks would help with reducing transition and down time between finding locations during the presentation. However, if you wanted each student to visit those curated locations from their own Google account in Google Earth on their personal devices, you would need to take this a step further:

For students to see your curated content, you will need to export that list as a KMZ file (FIGURE 6.9).

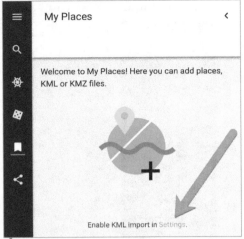

FIGURE 6.10

You can then share the file with your students by using Google Classroom or another online classroom environment. You could also put the KMZ into Google Drive and share it from there.

Your students will then take this file and import it into their Google Earth bookmarks.

To allow the importing and use of KML/KMZ files, students will need to toggle this setting to *on* in the Settings menu (FIGURE 6.10 and 6.11).

FIGURE 6.11

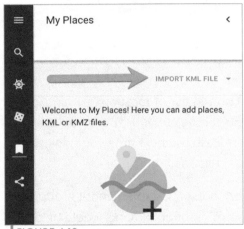

FIGURE 6.12

Once that setting has been turned on, the students are ready to take your KMZ file and import it into Google Earth. A user can import a file either from direct upload from the computer or by finding the file in Google Drive (FIGURE 6.12).

Share

While exploring Google Earth, you and your students can share locations by link, social media, or even straight to Google Classroom (FIGURE 6.13).

FIGURE 6.13

Do More with Earth Imagery

Google Earth provides a wealth of information to its users; however, there are tools and resources that can give Google Earth additional functionality within one's classroom. Let's look at some tools and sites that you can integrate with Google Earth to enhance student learning.

Earth Timelapse

The satellites that produce Google Earth's imagery are working hard all the time. Some of their captures over time have been transformed into visualizations and animations to demonstrate the changes taking place on Earth. Students can greatly benefit from seeing how our land is shifting and the rate at which change is happening. To learn more about Earth Timelapse, please visit: geotools.co/timelapse (FIGURE 6.14).

FIGURE 6.14

GE Teach

Josh Williams, a geography educator in Texas, created GETeach.com, a website that boasts several fantastic tools to integrate with Google Earth. One of the site's best features is the data comparison feature. It grants the ability to load public data sets into either side of the map. You can then ask your students questions to see if and how they can infer ideas from data, allowing you to make predictions and draw conclusions from the data they are seeing. For instance, this example shows oil reserves on the left map and population density on the right map. A question we might ask students is, "How do you think governments will have to negotiate the sharing of these natural resources? Who has the upper hand when it comes to some of these negotiations?"

For more information, please visit:

» geteach.com (FIGURE 6.15).

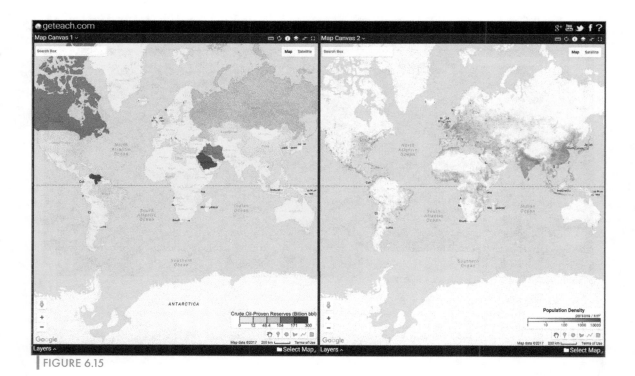

FIGURE 6.15

Google Lit Trips

Literature brings readers into different worlds, but sometimes readers can benefit from understanding geography, topography, and cultural details from a location in a book. Google Lit Trips is a website that provides teachers with KMZ files for various pieces of literature; for instance, if you were reading *The Odyssey* by Homer, you could download that particular KMZ file and then show your students where in the real world this story took place (FIGURE 6.16).

Since Jerome Burg started Google Lit Trips several years ago, the library of available KMZ files has grown. As a teacher, you will need to sign in and then fill out a small form on the website to receive the requested KMZ file. Once you have the file you can import it directly into Google Earth, the same way described in previous sections of this chapter.

For more information on how to use Google Lit Trips, please visit

» googlelittrips.org

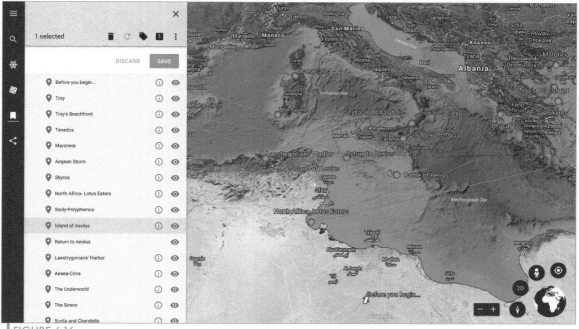

FIGURE 6.16

Google Earth Tools and Educational Content

Google Earth provides a wide array of experiences for our students. Take a moment to peruse the following additional functionalities for Google Earth. We keep an updated list of extension links and activities on our site.

Please see our **geotools.co/moreearth** site for direct links to the following projects:

» Google Earth Gallery—Contains collections of magnificent maps.

» Google Sky—View and explore the constellations.

» Google Earth Engine—See some truly amazing data representations in Google Earth.

» See the Heroes of Google Earth and how they are using it to change the world.

» One World, Many Stories—Choose a story and begin your journey.

» Google Earth Outreach—gives nonprofits and public benefit organizations the knowledge and resources they need to visualize their cause.

» Earth View Chrome Extension from Google Earth—Earth View displays a beautiful and unique Satellite image from Google Maps every time you open a new tab.

» EarthView—This one's for those who just want to explore.

» Fly anywhere with the Flight Simulator.

» Explore the Sky, the Moon and Mars.

» Google Earth Hacks—This links to interesting content found or created and provides quick access to check things out in Google Earth.

What You Can Do Tomorrow

Here are ideas of what you can do in your classroom tomorrow using Google Earth:

- » Explore a voyage with students, asking guiding questions.
- » Import a KML that you found through a web search, and guide students through a tour.
- » Search for a location to explore in new Google Earth.
- » Have them explore Google Earth using voyager with an inquiry-based activity, such as an A, E, I, O, U chart (A=adjective, E=emotion, I=interesting, O= Oh? Surprised by __, and U= Um, I still have a question about __).

"An understanding of the natural world and what's in it is a source of not only a great curiosity but great fulfillment."

—David Attenborough

CHAPTER 7:
Using Video as a Tool for Global Communication

So far in the book we have made and manipulated maps, immersed ourselves in imagery, built interactive tours, and traveled our planet through Google Earth. Now we'll explore ways to add the human voice, the narrative, and the inquiry-based conversation into your global classroom. In this section, we will explore Google Hangouts and Google+ Communities as tools that allow classrooms to connect. We will also explore YouTube and some of the content you can curate to deepen your students' understanding and perspective of our world.

Part of being a global citizen means that we have the ability to communicate and collaborate beyond our physical borders. With that being the case, the questions for educators become: *How do I do that with the resources I have? Where do I even begin?* Luckily, for years now, educators from around the world have been asking the same questions, finding solutions, and building communities in which they can find thinking partners, project collaborators, and sister classrooms with which to communicate.

GOOGLE HANGOUTS: An Overview

Google Hangouts is a video calling and messaging app. This app can be located through Gmail and Google+, as well as its own app (hangouts.google.com). With Hangouts, a teacher can create a video call wherein he or she can invite others to join.

Let's look at the features of Google Hangouts (FIGURE 7.1):

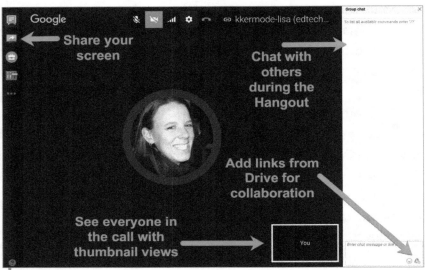

FIGURE 7.1

FIGURE 7.2

PRO TIP: If you are scheduling an interview with someone, you can create a Google Calendar event and add the Hangouts video call link directly to the event invite. That way everyone knows where to find the video call and how to enter the video chat (FIGURE 7.2).

Classroom Ideas

Here are some ideas of how teachers have used Google Hangouts and YouTube as classroom tools to foster global citizenship:

» Classroom-to-classroom video calls to play a Mystery Location Game

» Student-to-student video calls. After being pen pals for months, students are finally able to talk face-to-face.

» Video calls with an ambassador from another region and/or country

» Video calls with international organizations to spark conversation around environmental, political, and/or community-based topics

» Video calls with missionaries or charitable organizations to jumpstart a donation campaign. Students can speak with someone at "ground zero" in the area of need.

» Hangouts on Air, an option in YouTube Live, with experts (authors, environmentalists, etc.), wherein an interview or discussion takes place. Instead of that conversation being lost, the conversation can be published to YouTube for reference and shared with others once it's over.

» YouTube Live video tours of schools and/or classrooms to share with other classrooms in other parts of the world. This can be captured in flat screen or 360° video formats. YouTube links are easily shared via email.

Mystery Location Hangouts

One way to connect with others is through Mystery Location Hangouts. There is an entire Google+ Community focused on connecting classrooms with each other so students can gain geographic knowledge through an inquiry-based cycle (FIGURE 7.3).

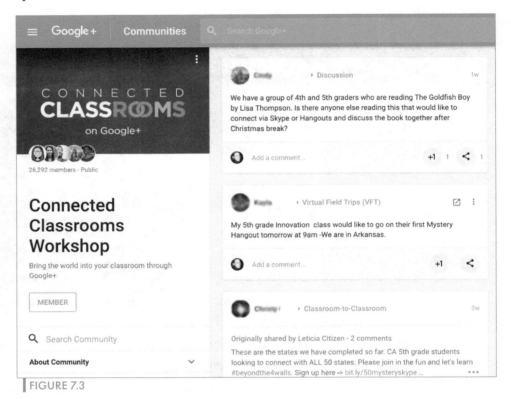

FIGURE 7.3

How It Works

A teacher posts to the community with which they would like to connect, providing details about where they are located, what age group, and potentially when they are hoping to have the hangout. Then other teachers looking to connect respond to the posting and plan a time and date for the hangout.

The "Mystery" part of this is that students from each class do not know the location of the class with whom they are speaking. On the day of the Hangout, the classes in both classrooms gather as a group in front of a webcam to meet each other. Then the questions begin. Students ask geographical and historical questions to get a sense of the region, state, and city in which the other classroom resides.

Mystery Hangouts allow students to build several key skills for global citizenship. First, it allows for direct conversation and interaction with others outside their own community, developing much needed communication skills. It also builds empathy. Not every classroom to which a class connects is going to look the same or provide the same environment. This experience fosters the idea that we are all learners, no matter where we are located, and while we may see differences, there is much more that makes us similar. Students will also be asking questions and synthesizing responses; this fosters critical thinking.

To learn more about the Mystery Location Hangouts, please visit:

» geotools.co/mysterycalls.

YouTube

In keeping with our goal of developing global citizens, we would feel remiss if we left out the single greatest repository of learning content in the world. YouTube was first publicly released in November of 2005, and has seen massive growth spikes in the past ten years. With more than three hundred hours of YouTube being uploaded every minute, the site is an invaluable source for globally created videos that can enhance any lesson.

There are several ways to curate content for viewing with your students on YouTube. If we are trying to foster empathy as part of our global citizenship skills, then being immersed in a 360° news story will develop that far better than would reading a flat news article. Many news outlets, including the *New York Times* and the *Washington Post*, are now publishing 360° news broadcasts and posting them to YouTube. This allows students not only to read updated news, it allows them to hear, see, and experience those stories in an immersive format.

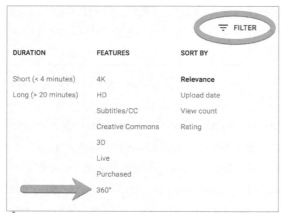

FIGURE 7.4

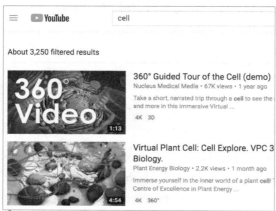

FIGURE 7.5

FIGURE 7.6

If you are interested in providing students with links or playlists to 360° content, you must first know how to search for it; for instance, if you wanted your students to actually go into a cell instead of just look at one, your search for that content in YouTube would be slightly different. The following steps would be required:

1. Open YouTube.

2. Type in *cell* into the search bar.

3. When you click enter, you will see a normal set of search results. Now we are going to look for the Filters (FIGURE 7.4).

4. Click on Filters and then choose 360°. This will limit the content to only 360° videos.

5. You should see several video options in 360° now (FIGURE 7.5). Choose one to view.

6. You can now click your cursor inside the video and drag around to see the entire 360° view (FIGURE 7.6).

7. Notice the sidebar of other suggested content. This is another great way to find additional 360° videos.

 If you would like to peruse other 360° playlists or have direct links to many of the 360° news outlets, please visit:

» geotools.co/360vids.

Connecting Your Classroom to the World: How to Broadcast Using YouTube Live

There may come a point when you would like to broadcast a class session live. Maybe you are having a Google Hangout with a guest speaker and would like to offer parents a lens into the conversation. Maybe you would like to record it and store it directly on YouTube following its conclusion.

While Google Hangouts is great for private virtual meetings, if you would like to capture that meeting or interview, you'll need to use YouTube Live. YouTube Live now incorporates Hangouts on Air (or broadcasted Hangouts) as part of its menu of live events.

For details on how to use YouTube Live, please visit: **geotools.co/ytlive.**

What You Can Do Tomorrow

Here are ideas of what you can do in your classroom tomorrow using Google Hangouts:

» Connect with another classroom in your building using Google Hangouts for a quick activity.

» Explore the mystery hangouts community and find a teacher/classroom with whom to build a collaborative project.

» Use the strategy Can You Guess My 2-1-4 before connecting with a mystery hangout class. Show your students 2 facts, 1 clue, and 4 images to build background knowledge about the location of the mystery hangout.

"Broad, wholesome, charitable views of men and things cannot be acquired by vegetating in one little corner of the earth all of one's lifetime."

—Mark Twain

CHAPTER 8:
Google Tools for Research

John is a middle school physics teacher who wanted to shift the way he taught a unit on engineering design, planning, and building. Wanting to give his students an opportunity to explore building design plans from a perspective of historical to modern, he headed to the Google Arts and Culture website and found primary source documents of drawings and plans for iconic structures around the world, such as the Sydney Opera House and the Eiffel Tower. John created a gallery of the images he wanted his students to explore and examine. Using Google Classroom, he assigned the gallery to his students. He also provided a graphic organizer he had created in Google Drawing for them to complete their investigation of building design plans.

Sometimes when working with data, the searching can feel overwhelming for both the teacher and the students. Thankfully, it doesn't have to be. As educators, it is our job to help our students learn how to sift through the world's information and develop communication and collaboration skills.

There are several open data sources from which your students can gather their information. We are aware that the web is always changing, and new resources are constantly created. Rather than list sites here that may be outdated in a few months, we maintain a current resource list on our website: geotools.co/data.

Create a SPREADSHEET

Once you and/or your students have found a data source that works with your learning objective, the goal is to get that data into Google Spreadsheets. Often a site will have a data table or embedded spreadsheet from which the students can pull their information. Table data can be copied and pasted right into a spreadsheet for further mapping and visualization. Simply click and drag your cursor to highlight the table and then click Copy. Open a spreadsheet in Google Sheets and then click Paste. The data should copy into cells the same way it appeared in the table on the site. Be sure to have your students keep a record of their cited sources while saving data to spreadsheets. For more information and examples, please visit: geotools.co/sheets

OPEN DATA KIT

Several years ago, Open Data Kit (ODK) was started by a small group of Google employees and interns. Their mission was to create an open source platform that would allow users to create tools, collect data, and make changes based on that data—anywhere in the world. The project is currently still being funded, and the team has grown in size and scope through the years.

ODK runs on the Android platform. There are tools for deploying large collection forms wherein the user can take snapshots, input quantitative and qualitative data, and click multiple-choice buttons for options. Due to circumstances in remote locations around the globe, a multitude of options are available for where and how to store the data off the devices. Once you have collected the data on a mobile device, you can use a local server or upload and store the data to an online domain.

 For more information on how ODK is being used, visit:

» opendatakit.org

The site hosts a wealth of information should you and/or your students decide to use mobile devices to collect data and work on a project for community growth.

GOOGLE ARTS AND CULTURE: An Overview

Launched in 2011, Google Arts and Culture is a lesser-known Internet gem which Google created. Partnering with museums and places of cultural and historical interest around the world, Google has curated high-quality images of works of art (paintings, drawings, statues, artifacts, primary source documents, images, etc.) and organized them into multiple easy-to-access categories. Since mid-2015 Google Arts and Culture has partnered with more than 850 organizations, has over 4.7 million media assets, and has more than 1,500 online exhibits—and its content continues to grow.

To get started, visit the Google Arts and Culture site: google.com/culturalinstitute (FIGURE 8.1). Sign in with your Google account. (In the upper right corner, you'll see your profile picture or the words *Sign In*.)

The homepage of Google Arts and Culture hosts featured content including featured stories, themes, collections, and highlighted Street View imagery. There are a number of ways to search through the Google Arts and Culture site using the navigation tools found in the menu. (It's under the three-bar icon up at the top of the page.) You and your students may notice that the menu is broken up

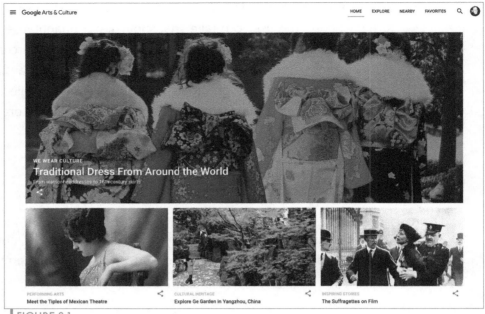

FIGURE 8.1

into three parts (similar to the Google Maps menu). The first section focuses on your curated content and what may be of interest near you geographically. The second section is for content organized broadly by collection or theme, and special experiments. And the third section hones in on particular artists, mediums, historical events, figures, and locations.

Here's a walkthrough of the individual menu items:

- » **Home**—Click to go back to the home page.
- » **Explore**—Highlights featured content.
- » **Nearby**—This is curated content based on current location.
- » **Profile**—Here you will find your favorites and created galleries.
- » **Collections**—This is curated content from museums and partners, also listed on an interactive map.
- » **Themes**—This is curated content based on various movements, cultures, and locations.
- » **Experiments**—This is where coders try and create interactions with art based on conditional formulas and algorithms.

» **Artists**—Search by individual artists.

» **Mediums**—Search by art medium (paper, canvas, photograph, etc.).

» **Art Movements**—Search by time periods in art history (modern art, impressionism, futurism).

» **Historical Events**—This is content organized into online exhibits by historical events.

» **Historical Figures**—This is content organized by historical figures.

» **Places**—This is content organized by countries and cities.

» **About**—Learn more about the Arts & Culture website & partners.

» **Send Feedback** —Share ideas and screenshots with Arts and Culture

Additionally, in the upper right corner of the site there is a search icon. Clicking it allows a user to search by a topic, artist, medium, historical figure or event, etc. This will search the site for all content related to the search term and display results organized by online exhibits, related items (images, videos, art, etc.), museum views (using Street View imagery), related topics, and user-created galleries (FIGURE 8.2).

FIGURE 8.2

The Google Arts and Culture team has started to use the state-of-the-art Art Camera that collects gigapixel images of works of art. This translates into amazing, high-quality images on which you can zoom in to see the finest details (like brush strokes) that we may not even get to see when visiting a museum in person (FIGURE 8.3).

Spend a few minutes exploring in the art project. Find an item you like and click on it to open it in a larger view. Open the zoom tool by clicking on the magnifying glass icon. The zoom in/out tool will appear on the right side. Use it to zoom in and then move around the image using your mouse/trackpad.

FIGURE 8.3

Creating Galleries

FIGURE 8.4

The Google Arts and Culture site makes it possible for users to create their own collections using the content within the site. Browsing the site and adding content to the Favorites section is an easy way to build a curated collection that you can share with others later. To save an item, find the heart icon (FIGURE 8.4). You will find the heart icon when viewing individual items. The heart icon will be on the upper right corner next to the share icon.

Once you have several items saved, you can use them to make a curated collection.

Click on the menu (three bars in the top left) and choose Favorites. Your favorited content can be found here. Above your individual content pieces there is an option to Create a new collection. Click on this button. The next step is to select which favorites you are going to put into this specific collection. Choose items. Then click Next. Give your new collection a name and description. Here you have the option to make your collection public. You will want to do this if you plan on sharing this with students. Click Finish. Your curated collection page now shows. It will show whether it is listed as public or private. There is also the option to edit and add more to the collection. To share the collection, click the share icon in the upper right corner and select where to share or copy the URL in the Chrome omnibox and paste it in an email, on a doc, or on a website.

PRO TIP: Share like a Pro. Within every collection, you have a share button. In the share button are several options. One of the best features of the Google Arts and Culture site is the ability to share directly to Google Classroom. You can share your custom collection as well as already-curated collections and content directly to Google Classroom (FIGURE 8.5). Your custom collection remains completely editable. When editing the collection, you can add or remove content and change the title or description as well as the privacy

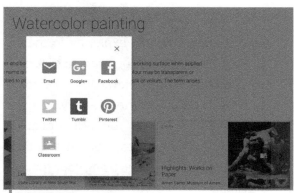

FIGURE 8.5

settings. As you finish editing your collection, it shows you the collection view as it will appear to your students when shared. This view also allows you to grab the link by copying/pasting it from the address bar when viewing the collection.

Sharing a Gallery or Item

When viewing a gallery, item, or listing, you'll see a share icon below the item. When you click on it, you will see the various ways to share: G+, Facebook, Twitter, Google Classroom, Email, Tumblr, and even Pinterest. To find the link to your gallery, head up to the address bar, copy the link, and paste it.

It is also possible to share the link to individual works of art from the Google Arts and Culture site. Any item that has the share link icon can be shared in the same way.

Instructional Ideas

As described above, the Google Arts and Culture site is rich with resources, which lends itself to many lesson ideas; for example, students can become "curators" and create a collection or "online exhibit" centered around a theme, topic, or time period in art and/or history determined by teachers or students. Students can then share their collections in the form of a gallery walk around the classroom, listing questions/instructions for their peers to navigate and from which they can gain new knowledge and/or ask further questions. Another idea is to use Google Arts and Culture imagery for writing prompts. Students could compare two authors or discuss an author's purpose for writing a modern-day story inspired by a historical image or piece of artwork. Additionally, a scavenger hunt or "Amazing Race" makes for a fun and active learning activity. These include clues and questions through which students work to solve a problem or answer an essential question centered around the content in the Google Arts and Culture site.

We hope this sparks a few ideas for instructional uses of the Google Arts and Culture site. For even more ideas, please visit: geotools.co/GAClessons.

What You Can Do Tomorrow

Here are ideas of what you can do in your classroom tomorrow using Google Arts and Culture:

» Pick two pieces of art and have your students compare and contrast the artwork. Use a Venn Diagram as a graphic organizer for students to use while finding what's similar and different.

» Pick a location from the Places menu option, and have your students explore that place through its art and culture.

» From the Cultures menu option, have students pick a topic or theme, and analyze how we got to where we are today through the influences of others.

"Be the change you wish to see in the world."

—Gandhi

Final Thoughts

Well, we've come to the end of our book, but don't think we're finished! If you have enjoyed this journey, learned a few things along the way, immersed your students in new worlds, and explored various ways to increase the presence of cultures and art in your classroom, then you are on the right path!

We plan to keep sharing the latest and greatest geo tools and classroom uses with you for years to come. Please visit our website, CreateGlobalLearners.com, to find additional tips, tricks, and resources.

Feel free to reach out to us if you have any questions regarding the content or ideas in this book or if you have ideas you need help hashing through to fruition. We love to work with new ideas and bring them to life.

Thank you so much for spending time between the pages with us. We'll see you again soon.

—Kelly and Kim

ACKNOWLEDGMENTS

From Kelly

I would like to take a moment and acknowledge a few people without whom I may have never taken so many leaps in the past several years. Thank you to Linda for being a mentor and friend with the fewest words. Sometimes all it took was a nod, and I knew. A big thanks to Matt. Teamwork makes the dream work. Thanks for the continuous journey of growth together. Thank you to Andy, for honest feedback and support at any hour. Thanks to Kris for the careful eye and edits. Your hours and support are appreciated. Thanks to the eAchieve team for allowing me to be a part of a truly amazing group of educators. Thank you to Dan Behm and FHPS for supporting me.

My colleagues, near and far, you are my *framily*. Thank you for the shared learning experiences over the past eighteen years. I am truly blessed to work with amazing staff every day of my career. We get to push each other to improve our best practices, expect excellence and risk taking from one another, and have a great time in the process. I look forward to continuing this wild ride for years to come.

To my students: For many years, my classroom was a place wherein my students and I pushed each other to improve all the time. I'd like to thank Jeff and Lisa, who said I had "two years." I owe you both. I'd also like to thank the following students from whom I learned far more than I could ever repay: ND, YK, HC, EM, HM, EB, MB, MP, EJ, TA, SM, SD, SJ, KD, and LM.

Kim, Thanks for being a fantastic co-writer and teammate. From our weeks in Natrona running workshops together to gallivanting New Orleans together, our friendship was founded on our mutual passion for exploring the world. What a wonderful journey it has been to write this book with you.

Thank you to Holly Clark and EdTechTeam for taking leaps with Kim and me. We are most grateful.

From Kim

To the educators and students: Thank you for the opportunity to share, learn, explore, and grow with you over the years. My journey in teaching with educational technology began at Isidore Newman School in New Orleans, LA, which at the time was already implementing educational technology. This teaching experience enhanced my career and passion for educational technology and became the launch pad that has led to every opportunity to learn and grow as an educator in the field of educational technology. I will forever be grateful.

My colleagues, PLN near and far, you are the best. I am blessed to know you, work with you, and learn from you on a daily basis!

To the Google Earth Education Outreach team, Google Earth Education Advisory Board, and Google Geo Teachers Institute team: It's always a blast to work with you, and you all are very much a part of the inspiration for our book. Thank you!

To Will Byington (willbyington.com) for your fabulous photography skills.

To my mom for your amazing editing skills, thank you!

Kelly, what a journey! Thank you for taking this idea and running with it. Thank you for your dedication, hard work, and friendship! Here's to many more years of friendship, working together, and exploring the globe.

Special thanks to EdTechTeam and Holly Clark for giving us this opportunity to write, publish, and share our passion for geo tools. We are grateful!

Want to Create More Global Learning Opportunities?

Here are ways to stay connected:

1. Host a Workshop at Your School

   » Bring the World to Your Classroom MasterClass—Create and Customize Learning for Your Classroom (one-day) edtechteam.press/masterclass.

   » Engage Me!—How to Design Lessons Using Google's Geo Tools.

   » Private Label—We will customize a workshop to fit your school's needs.

2. Take the Online Course

   » Creating Global Learners with Geo Tools

3. Attend an EdTechTeam Summit featuring Google for Education.

4. Schedule a Global Learners Keynote.

5. Join the Google Earth Education Community. google.com/earth/education.

For more information visit EdTechTeam.com/press.

To request a workshop or for more info, contact press@edtechteam.com

CreateGlobalLearners.com

#GeoClassroom

More Books from EdTechTeam Press
edtechteam.com/books

The HyperDoc Handbook
Digital Lesson Design Using Google Apps
By Lisa Highfill, Kelly Hilton, and Sarah Landis

The HyperDoc Handbook is a practical reference guide for all K–12 educators who want to transform their teaching into blended-learning environments. *The HyperDoc Handbook* is a bestselling book that strikes the perfect balance between pedagogy and how-to tips while also providing ready-to-use lesson plans to get you started with HyperDocs right away.

Innovate with iPad
Lessons to Transform Learning
By Karen Lirenman and Kristen Wideen

Written by two primary teachers, this book provides a complete selection of clearly explained, engaging, open-ended lessons to change the way you use iPad with students at home or in the classroom. It features downloadable task cards, student-created examples, and extension ideas to use with your students. Whether you have access to one iPad for your entire class or one for each student, these lessons will help you transform learning in your classroom.

The Space
A Guide for Educators

By Rebecca Louise Hare and Robert Dillon

The Space supports the conversation around a revolution happening in education today concerning the reshaping of school spaces. This book goes well beyond the ideas for learning-space design that focuses on Pinterest-perfect classrooms and instead discusses real and practical ways to design learning spaces that support and drive learning.

A Learner's Paradise
How New Zealand Is Reimagining Education

By Richard Wells

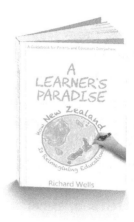

What if teachers were truly trusted to run education? In *A Learner's Paradise*, Richard Wells outlines New Zealand's forward-thinking education system in which teachers are empowered to do exactly that. With no prescribed curriculum, teachers and students work together to create individualized learning plans—all the way through the high school level. From this guidebook, you'll learn how New Zealand is reimagining education and setting an example for innovative educators, parents, and school districts to follow.

Classroom Management in the Digital Age
Effective Practices for Technology-Rich Learning Spaces

By Patrick Green and Heather Dowd

Classroom Management in the Digital Age helps guide and support teachers through the new landscape of device-rich classrooms. It provides practical strategies to novice and expert educators alike who want to maximize learning and minimize distraction. Learn how to keep up with the times while limiting time wasters and senseless screen-staring time.

The Google Apps Guidebook
Lessons, Activities, and Projects Created by
Students for Teachers
By Kern Kelley and the Tech Sherpas

The Google Apps Guidebook is filled with great ideas for the classroom from the voices of the students themselves. Each chapter introduces an engaging project that teaches students (and teachers) how to use one of Google's powerful tools. Projects are differentiated for a variety of age ranges and can be adapted for most content areas.

Dive into Inquiry
Amplify Learning and Empower Student Voice
By Trevor MacKenzie

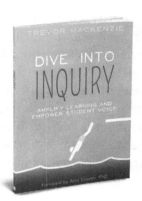

Dive into Inquiry beautifully marries the voice and choice of inquiry with the structure and support required to optimize learning. With *Dive into Inquiry* you'll gain an understanding of how to best support your learners as they shift from a traditional learning model into an inquiry classroom where student agency is fostered and celebrated each and every day.

Sketchnotes for Educators
100 Inspiring Illustrations for Lifelong Learners
By Sylvia Duckworth

Sketchnotes for Educators contains 100 of Sylvia Duckworth's most popular sketchnotes, with links to the original downloads that can be used in class or shared with colleagues. Interspersed throughout the book are reflections from Sylvia about what motivated her to create the drawings as well as commentary from many of the educators whose work inspired her sketchnotes.

Code in Every Class
How All Educators Can Teach Programming
By Kevin Brookhouser and Ria Megnin

In *Code in Every Class*, Kevin Brookhouser and Ria Megnin explain why computer science is critical to your students' future success. With lesson ideas and step-by-step instruction, they show you how to take tech education into your own hands and open a world of opportunities to your students. And here's the best news: You *don't* have to be a computer genius to teach the basics of coding.

Making Your School Something Special
Enhance Learning, Build Confidence, and Foster Success at Every Level
By Rushton Hurley

In *Making Your School Something Special*, educator and international speaker Rushton Hurley explores the mindsets, activities, and technology that make for great learning. You'll learn how to create strong learning activities and make your school a place where students and teachers alike want to be—because it's where they feel energized, inspired and *special*.

The Google Cardboard Book
Explore, Engage, and Educate with Virtual Reality
An EdTechTeam Collaboration

In *The Google Cardboard Book*, EdTechTeam trainers and leaders offer step-by-step instructions on how to use virtual reality technology in your classroom—no matter what subject you teach. You'll learn what tools you need (and how affordable they can be), which apps to start with, and how to view, capture, and share 360° videos and images.

Transforming Libraries
A Toolkit for Innovators, Makers, and Seekers
By Ron Starker

In the Digital Age, it's more important than ever for libraries to evolve into gathering points for collaboration, spaces for innovation, and places where authentic learning occurs. In *Transforming Libraries*, Ron Starker reveals ways to make libraries makerspaces, innovation centers, community commons, and learning design studios that engage multiple forms of intelligence.

Intention
Critical Creativity in the Classroom
By Amy Burvall and Dan Ryder

Inspiring and exploring creativity opens pathways for students to use creative expression to demonstrate content knowledge, critical thinking, and the problem solving that will serve them best no matter what their futures may bring. *Intention* offers a collection of ideas, activities, and reasons for bringing creativity to every lesson.

Making Your Teaching Something Special
50 Simple Ways to Become a Better Teacher
By Rushton Hurley

In the second book in his series, Rushton Hurley highlights key areas of teaching that play a part in shaping your success as an educator. Whether you are finding your way as a brand new teacher or are a seasoned teacher who is looking for some powerful ideas, this book offers inspiration and practical advice to help you make this year your best yet.

The Google Infused Classroom
A Guidebook to Making Thinking Visible and Amplifying Student Voice
By Holly Clark and Tanya Avrith

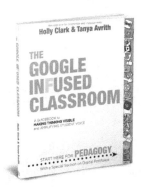

This beautifully designed book offers guidance on using technology to design instruction that allows students to show their thinking, demonstrate their learning, and share their work (and voices!) with authentic audiences. *The Google Infused Classroom* will equip you to empower your students to use technology in meaningful ways that prepare them for the future.

The Conference Companion
Sketchnotes, Doodles, and Creative Play for Teaching and Learning
By Becky Green

Wherever you are learning, whatever your doodle comfort level, this jovial notebook is your buddy. Grab a pencil, pen, crayon, or quill. Sketchnotes, doodles, and creative play await both you and your students. Part workshop, part journal, and part sketchbook, these simple and light-hearted scaffolds and lessons will transform your listening and learning experiences while providing creative inspiration for your classroom.

50 Ways to Use YouTube In the Classroom
By Patrick Green

Your students are already accessing YouTube, so why not meet them where they are as consumers of information? By using the tools they choose, you can maximize their understanding in ways that matter. *50 Ways to Use YouTube in the Classroom* is an accessible guide that will improve your teaching, your students' learning, and your classroom culture.

ABOUT THE AUTHORS

Kelly Kermode currently serves as an Integrated Learning Specialist for Forest Hills Public Schools in Grand Rapids, Michigan. With over 20 years of teaching and coaching experience, Kelly loves to think big and explore ways to think outside the box. Over her teaching career Kelly has taught over 17 different classes, including English, health, economics, algebra, computer information systems, web design, app development, tools for learning, AP computer science, and yearbook journalism. From Bolivia to California to Michigan to South Africa, Kelly loves to share her love for global education and infusing geo-literacy into all subjects. She leads workshops, provides coaching, conducts Google Bootcamps, and facilitates custom professional development for several entities including Forest Hills Public Schools, EdTechTeam, MACUL, CUE, ISTE, and EdTech Summit SA. Kelly is a member of the Google Earth Education Advisory Board, Google Certified Innovator and Trainer, CUE Lead Learner, Adobe Education Leader, Adobe Certified Expert, and Adobe Education Trainer. Kelly earned her B.A. in English Literature and Philosophy from Francis Marion University and her Masters in Ed. with Special Education endorsement from Aquinas College. Kelly is the proud mother to two children, Tynan and Madeleine. In her free time, Kelly enjoys reading, cooking, throwing pottery, and gardening.

 kellykermode.com

 @coachk

 kkermode@gmail.com

 plus.google.com/+KellyKermode

Kim Randall, a global educational technology consultant, works with professional development organizations such as EdTechTeam, Discovery Education and the Krause Center for Innovation, providing relevant and engaging training centered around effective use and pedagogy of educational technologies in the classroom. She is a Google Certified Innovator, Trainer and an Apple Distinguished Educator, earned a B.A. in Psychology and Early Childhood Education at Tulane University in New Orleans, LA, and an M.A. in Educational Technology Leadership from George Washington University in Washington D.C. She is a member of the Google Earth Education Advisory Board and currently a cohort lead for the western region. Kim is actively involved with the Google Geo Teacher's Institute and continues to present geo-literacy related sessions at conferences, Google for Education summits, workshops, and bootcamps around the globe. She has been an elementary and middle school teacher as well as a technology integration specialist and holds a California Multiple Subject teaching credential. She is based in the San Francisco Bay Area, but often found in her spare time traveling to new places near and far, scuba diving, and dabbling with topside and underwater photography.

 creategloballearners.com   @scubagirl812

 kimster812@gmail.com   plus.google.com/+KimRandall